P9-CRZ-090

THE REAL THING

A Comedy in Two Acts

by
Tom Stoppard

SAMUEL FRENCH, INC.

45 West 25th Street   NEW YORK 10010
7623 Sunset Boulevard HOLLYWOOD 90046
LONDON   TORONTO

Copyright © 1982,1983, 1984 by Tom Stoppard

ALL RIGHTS RESERVED

CAUTION: Professionals and amateurs are hereby warned that THE REAL THING is subject to a royalty. It is fully protected under the copyright laws of the United States of America, the British Commonwealth, including Canada, and all other countries of the Copyright Union. All rights, including professional, amateur, motion pictures, recitation, lecturing, public reading, radio broadcasting, television, and the rights of translation into foreign languages are strictly reserved. In its present form the play is dedicated to the reading public only.

The amateur live stage performance rights to THE REAL THING are controlled exclusively by Samuel French, Inc., and royalty arrangements and licenses must be secured well in advance of presentation. PLEASE NOTE that amateur royalty fees are set upon application in accordance with your producing circumstances. When applying for a royalty quotation and license please give us the number of performances intended, dates of production, your seating capacity and admission fee. Royalties are payable one week before the opening performance of the play to Samuel French, Inc., at 45 West 25th Street, New York, NY 10010-2751; or at 7623 Sunset Blvd., Hollywood, CA 90046-2795, or to Samuel French (Canada), Ltd., 100 Lombard Street, Toronto, Ontario, Canada M5C 1M3.

Royalty of the required amount must be paid whether the play is presented for charity or gain and whether or not admission is charged.

Stock royalty quoted on application to Samuel French, Inc.

For all other rights than those stipulated above, apply to Fraser & Dunlop (Scripts) Ltd., Chelsea Harbour, Lots Road; Fifth floor, The Chambers; London SW10 OXF, England.

Particular emphasis is laid on the question of amateur or professional readings, permission and terms for which must be secured in writing from Samuel French, Inc.

Copying from this book in whole or in part is strictly forbidden by law, and the right of performance is not transferable.

Whenever the play is produced the following notice must appear on all programs, printing and advertising for the play: "Produced by special arrangement with Samuel French, Inc."

Due authorship credit must be given on all programs, printing and advertising for the play.

No one shall commit or authorize any act or omission by which the copyright of, or the right to copyright, this play may be impaired.

No one shall make any changes in this play for the purpose of production.

Publication of this play does not imply availability for performance. Both amateurs and professionals considering a production are *strongly* advised in their own interests to apply to Samuel French, Inc., for the written permission before starting rehearsals, advertising, or booking a theatre.

No part of this book may be reproduced, stored in a retrieval system, or transmitted in any form, by any means, now known or yet to be invented, including mechanical, electronic, photocopying, recording, videotaping, or otherwise, without the prior written permission of the publisher.

ISBN 0 573 61458 X   Printed in U.S.A.

For Miriam

STRAND THEATRE
ALDWYCH, LONDON, WC2

Proprietors: Strand Theatre Limited
President: Enid Chanelle
Chairman: Arnold M. Crook
Managing Director: Anthony Peek
A Member of the Louis I. Michaels Ltd Group

MICHAEL CODRON
presents

FELICITY KENDAL   ROGER REES

in

TOM STOPPARD'S
new play
THE REAL THING
with
POLLY ADAMS
JEREMY CLYDE

MICHAEL THOMAS SUZANNA HAMILTON IAN OLIVER

Directed by
PETER WOOD
Lighting by
WILLIAM BUNDY
Designed by
CARL TOMS

Sound Design by
JONATHAN DEANS

Costume Supervisor
BRUCE SNYDER

Associate Producer
DAVID SUTTON

First performance at the Strand Theatre, Tuesday 16, November 1982

CAST IN ORDER OF APPEARANCE

Max	JEREMY CLYDE
Charlotte	POLLY ADAMS
Henry	ROGER REES
Annie	FELICITY KENDAL
Billy	MICHAEL THOMAS
Debbie	SUZANNA HAMILTON
Brodie	IAN OLIVER

There will be one interval of fifteen minutes. Two years elapse between Acts I and II.

Gerald Schoenfeld, *Chairman*   Bernard B. Jacobs, *President*

EMANUEL AZENBERG, THE SHUBERT ORGANIZATION, ICARUS PRODUCTIONS
BYRON GOLDMAN, IVAN BLOCH, ROGER BERLIND and MICHAEL CODRON
present

JEREMY IRONS   GLENN CLOSE

in

THE REAL THING

by

TOM STOPPARD

also starring

CHRISTINE BARANSKI   KENNETH WELSH

CYNTHIA NIXON   PETER GALLAGHER   VYTO RUGINIS

Scenery by   Costumes by   Lighting by
TONY WALTON   ANTHEA SYLBERT   THARON MUSSER
General Manager   Sound by   Production Supervisor
JOSE VEGA   OTTS MUNDERLOH   MARTIN HERZER

Directed by

MIKE NICHOLS

THE REAL THING was originally produced in London by Michael Codron
The Producers and Theatre Management are Members
of The League of New York Theatres and Producers, Inc.

Cast In Order Of Appearance

Max	KENNETH WELSH
Charlotte	CHRISTINE BARANSKI
Henry	JEREMY IRONS
Annie	GLENN CLOSE
Billy	PETER GALLAGHER
Debbie	CYNTHIA NIXON
Brodie	VYTO RUGINIS

Two years elapse between Acts I and II.

STANDBYS

Standbys never substitute for a listed player unless a specific
announcement is made at the time of the performance.
For Henry/Max—EDMOND GENEST; for Annie/Charlotte—LESLIE LYLES;
for Debbie—YEARDLEY SMITH; for Billy/Brodie—TODD WARING.

CHARACTERS

MAX, 40-ish
CHARLOTTE, 35-ish
HENRY, 40-ish
ANNIE, 30-ish
BILLY, 22-ish
DEBBIE, 17
BRODIE, 25

PLEASE NOTE: the text of *The Real Thing* refers to numerous pieces of copyrighted music, suggesting their use in production of the play. Permission to produce *The Real Thing* does *not* include permission to use any of this music in production. This permission ought to be procured from the various copyright owners of the music.

THE REAL THING

ACT ONE
Scene One

MAX doesn't have to be physically impressive, but you wouldn't want him for an enemy. CHARLOTTE doesn't have to be especially attractive, but you instantly want her for a friend.

Living-room. Architects drawing board, perhaps. A partly open door leads to an unseen hall and an unseen front door. One or two other doors to other rooms.

MAX is alone, sitting in a comfortable chair, with a glass of wine and an open bottle to hand. He is using a pack of playing cards to build a pyramidical, tiered viaduct on the coffee table in front of him. He is about to add a pair of playing cards (leaning against each other to hold each other up), and the pyramid is going well. Beyond the door to the hall, the front door is heard being opened with a key. The light from there changes as the unseen front door is opened. MAX does not react to the opening of the door, which is more behind him than in front of him.

MAX. Don't slam—

(The front door slams, not violently. The viaduct of cards collapses.)

MAX. *(superfluously, philosophically)* …the door.

(CHARLOTTE, in the hall, wearing a topcoat, looks round the door just long enough to say two words and disappear again.)

CHARLOTTE. It's me. *(MAX leaves the cards where they have fallen. He takes a drink from the glass. He doesn't look up at all. CHARLOTTE, without the topcoat, comes back into the room carrying a small suitcase and a plastic duty-free airport bag. She puts the case down and comes up behind MAX's chair and kisses the top of his head.)*

CHARLOTTE. Hello.

MAX. Hello, lover.

CHARLOTTE. That's nice. You used to call me lover. *(She drops the airport bag on his lap and returns towards the suitcase.)*

MAX. Oh, it's you. I thought it was my lover. *(He doesn't look at his present. He puts the bag on the floor by his chair.)* Where is it you've been?

CHARLOTTE. *(The question surprises her. She is deflected from picking up her suitcase — presumably to take it into the bedroom — and the case remains where it is.)* Well, Switzerland, of course. Weren't you listening?

MAX. *(Finally looks at her.)* You look well. Done you good.

CHARLOTTE. What, since yesterday?

MAX. Well, something has. How's Ba'l?

CHARLOTTE. Who?

MAX. *(Affects to puzzle very briefly over her answer.)* I meant Ba'l. Do you say 'Basel'? I say Ba'l.

CHARLOTTE. Oh ... yes. I say Basel.

MAX. *(lilts)* 'Let's call the whole thing off...'

CHARLOTTE. *(Studies him briefly, quizzically.)* Fancy a drink? *(She notes the glass, the bottle and his behaviour. Pointedly, but affectionately.)* Another drink? *(He smiles at her, empties his glass and holds it up for her. She takes the glass, finds a second glass, pours wine into both glasses and gives MAX his own glass.)*

MAX. How's old Basel, then? Keeping fit?

CHARLOTTE. Are you a tiny bit sloshed?

MAX. Certainly.

CHARLOTTE. I didn't go to Basel.

MAX. *(discreetly but definitely interested by that)* No? Where did you go, then?

CHARLOTTE. Geneva.

MAX. *(Surprised, he cackles.)* Geneva! *(He drinks from his glass.)* How's old Geneva, then? Franc doing well?

CHARLOTTE. Who?

MAX. *(He affects surprise.)* The Swiss franc. Is it doing well?

CHARLOTTE. Are you all right?

MAX. Absolutely.

CHARLOTTE. How have you got on?

MAX. Not bad. My best was eleven pairs on the bottom row, but I ran out of cards.

CHARLOTTE. What about the thing you were working

on? ... What is it?

MAX. An hotel.

CHARLOTTE. Yes. You were two elevators short.

MAX. I've cracked it.

CHARLOTTE. Good.

MAX. I'm turning the whole place on its side and making it a bungalow. I still have a problem with the rooftop pool. As far as I can see, all the water is going to fall into the shallow end. How's the lake, by the way?

CHARLOTTE. What lake?

MAX. *(He affects surprise.)* Lake Geneva. You haven't been to Loch Ness, have you? Lake Geneva. It is at Geneva? It must be. They wouldn't call it Lake Geneva if it was at Ba'l or Basel. They'd call it Lake Ba'l or Basel. You know the Swiss. Utterly reliable. And they've done it without going digital, that's what I admire so much. They know it's all a snare and a delusion. I can remember digitals when they first came out. You had to give your wrist a vigorous shake like bringing down a thermometer, and the only place you could buy one was Tokyo. But *I* looked all over for the fifteen-jewelled movement. Men ran through the market place shouting, "The cog is dead." But still the Swiss didn't panic. In fact, they made a few digitals themselves, as a feint to draw the Japanese further into the mire, and got on with numbering the bank accounts. And now you see how the Japs are desperately putting hands on their digital watches. It's yodelling in the dark. They can yodel till the cows come home. The days of the digitals are numbered. The metaphor is built into them like a self-destruct mechanism. Mark my words, I was right about the skateboard, I was right about *nouvelle cuisine*, and I'll be proved right about the digital watch. Digitals have no class, you see. They're science and technology. Makes nonsense of a decent pair of cufflinks, as the Swiss are the first to understand. Good sale?

CHARLOTTE. *(Stares at him.)* What?

MAX. *(He affects surprise.)* Good sale. Was the sale good? The sale in Geneva, how was it? Did it go well in Geneva, the sale?

CHARLOTTE. What's the matter?

MAX. I'm showing an interest in your work. I thought you liked me showing an interest in your work. *My* showing. Save the gerund and screw the whale. Yes, I'm sure you do. I remember how cross you got when I said to someone, 'My wife works for Sotheby's or Christie's, I forget which.' You misjudged me, as it happens. You thought I was being smart at your expense. In fact, I had forgotten. How's old Christie, by the way? *(Strikes his forehead.)* There I go. How's old Sothers, by the way? Happy with the Geneva sale, I trust?

CHARLOTTE. *(Puts her glass down and moves to stand facing him. To call a halt.)* All right.

MAX. Just all right? Well, that's the bloody Swiss for you. Conservative, you see. The Japs could show them a thing or two. They'd have a whaling fleet in Lake Geneva by now. How's the skiing, by the way? Plenty of snow?

CHARLOTTE. Stop it — stop it — stop it. What have I done?

MAX. You forgot your passport.

CHARLOTTE. I did what?

MAX. You went to Switzerland without your passport.

CHARLOTTE. What makes you think that?

MAX. I found it in your recipe drawer.

CHARLOTTE. *(quietly)* Jesus God.

MAX. Quite.

CHARLOTTE. *(Moves away and looks at him with some curiosity.)* What were you looking for?

MAX. Your passport.

CHARLOTTE. It's about the last place I would have looked.

MAX. It was.

CHARLOTTE. Why were you looking for it?

MAX. I didn't know it was going to be your passport. If you see what I mean.

CHARLOTTE. I think I do. You go through my things when I'm away? *(pause, puzzled)* Why?

MAX. I liked it when I found nothing. You should have just put it in your handbag. We'd still be an ideal couple. So to speak.

CHARLOTTE. Wouldn't you have checked to see if it had been stamped?

MAX. That's a very good point. I notice that you never went to Amsterdam when you went to Amsterdam. I must say I take my hat off to you, coming home with Rembrandt place mats for your mother. It's those little touches that lift adultery out of the moral arena and make it a matter of style.

CHARLOTTE. I wouldn't go on, if I were you.

MAX. Rembrandt place mats! I wonder who's got the originals. Some Arab, is it? 'Dinner's ready, Abdul, put the Rembrandts on the table.'

CHARLOTTE. It's like when we were burgled. The same violation. Worse.

MAX. I'm not a burglar. I'm your husband.

CHARLOTTE. As I said. Worse.

MAX. Well, I'm sorry. I think I just apologized for finding out that you've deceived me. Yes, I did. How does she do it? *(She moves away, to leave the room.)* Are you going somewhere?

CHARLOTTE. I'm going to bed.

MAX. Aren't you going to tell me who it is?

CHARLOTTE. Who what is?

MAX. Your lover, lover.

CHARLOTTE. Which lover?

MAX. I assumed there'd only be the one.

CHARLOTTE. Did you?

MAX. Well, do you see them separately or both together? Sorry, that's not fair. Well, tell you what, nod your head if it's separately. *(She looks at him.)* Heavens. If you have an opening free, I'm not doing much at the moment. Or is the position taken? It is only two, is it? Nod your head. *(She looks at him.)* Golly, you are a dark horse. How do they all three get away at the same time? Do they work together, like the Marx Brothers? I'm not upsetting you, I hope?

CHARLOTTE. You underestimate me.

MAX. *(interested)* Do I? A string quartet, you mean? That sort of thing? *(He ponders for a moment.)* What does the fourth one do? *(She raises her hand.)* Got it. Plays by himself. You can slap me if you like. I won't slap you back. I abhor cliché. It's one of the things that has kept me faithful.

CHARLOTTE. *(Returns to the hall and reappears wearing her topcoat.)* If you don't mind, I think I will go out after all. *(She moves to close the door behind her.)*

MAX. You've forgotten your suitcase.

CHARLOTTE. *(Pause. She comes back and picks up the suitcase. She takes the case to the door.)* I'm sorry if you've had a bad time. But you've done everything wrong. There's a right thing to say if you can think what it is. *(She waits a moment.)*

MAX. *(thinks)* Is it anyone I know?

CHARLOTTE. You aren't anyone I know. *(She goes out, closing the door.)*

(The front door is heard opening and closing. MAX remains seated. After a moment he reaches down for the airport bag, puts it back on his lap and looks inside it. He starts to laugh. He withdraws from the bag a miniature Alp in a glass bowl. He gives the bowl a shake and creats a snowstorm within it. Then the snowstorm envelops the stage. Music — a pop record — makes a bridge to the next scene.)

Scene Two

*HENRY is amiable but can take care of himself. CHARLOTTE is
less amiable and can take even better care of herself. MAX is
nice, seldom assertive, conciliatory. ANNIE is very much like
the woman whom CHARLOTTE has ceased to be.*

*A living room. A record player and shelves of records. Sun-
day newspapers. The music is coming from the record player.
HENRY, with several record sleeves around him is searching for a particular piece of music. There are doors to hall,
kitchen, bedroom. CHARLOTTE enters barefoot, wearing
HENRY's dressing-gown which is too big for her. She is
unkempt from sleep and seems generally disordered.
HENRY looks up briefly.*

HENRY. Hello.

CHARLOTTE. *(Moves forward without answering, sits down
and looks around in a hopeless way.)* Oh, God.

HENRY. I thought you'd rather lie in. Do you want
some coffee?

CHARLOTTE. I don't know. *(Possibly referring to the litter of
record sleeves, wanly.)* What a mess.

HENRY. Don't worry ... don't worry... *(He continues to
search among the records.)*

CHARLOTTE. I think I'll just stay in bed.

15

HENRY. Actually, I phoned Max.

CHARLOTTE. What? Why?

HENRY. He was on my conscience. He's coming round.

CHARLOTTE. *(quite strongly)* I don't want to see *him*.

HENRY. Sorry.

CHARLOTTE. Honestly, Henry.

HENRY. Hang on — I think I've found it. *(He removes the pop record, which might have come to its natural end by now, from the record player and puts a different record on. Meanwhile—)*

CHARLOTTE. Are you still doing your list?

HENRY. Mmm.

CHARLOTTE. Have you got a favourite book?

HENRY. *Finnegans Wake.*

CHARLOTTE. Have you read it?

HENRY. Don't be silly. *(He lowers the arm onto the record and listens to a few bars of alpine Strauss — or sub-Strauss. Then he lifts the arm again.)* No … No … Damnation. *(He starts to put the record away.)* Do you remember when we were in some place like Bournemouth or Deauville, and there was an open-air dance floor right outside our window?

CHARLOTTE. No.

HENRY. Yes you do, I was writing my Jean-Paul Sartre play, and there was this bloody orchestra which kept coming back to the same tune every twenty minutes, so I started shouting out of the window and the hotel manager—

CHARLOTTE. That was St. Moritz. *(scornfully)* Bournemouth.

HENRY. Well, what was it?

CHARLOTTE. What was what?

HENRY. What was the tune called? It sounded like

Strauss or somebody.

CHARLOTTE. How does it go?

HENRY. I don't know, do I?

CHARLOTTE. Who were you with in Bournemouth?

HENRY. Don't mess about. I'm supposed to give them my eight records tomorrow, and so far I've got five and *Finnegans Wake*.

CHARLOTTE. Well, if you don't know what it's called and you can't remember how it goes, why in Christ's name do you want it on your desert island?

HENRY. It's not supposed to be eight records you love and adore.

CHARLOTTE. Yes, it is.

HENRY. It is not. It's supposed to be eight records you associate with turning-points in your life.

CHARLOTTE. Well, I'm a turning-point in your life, and when you took me to St. Moritz your favourite record was the Ronettes doing 'Da Doo Ron Ron'.

HENRY. The Crystals. *(scornfully)* The Ronettes.

CHARLOTTE. *(Gets up and during the following searches, successfully, for a record, which she ends up putting on the machine.)* You're going about this the wrong way. Just pick your eight all-time greats and then remember what you were doing at the time. What's wrong with that?

HENRY. I'm supposed to be one of your intellectual playwrights. I'm going to look a total prick, aren't I, going on the radio to announce that while I was telling Jean-Paul Sartre that he was essentially superficial, I was spending the whole time listening to the Crystals singing 'Da Doo Ron Ron'. Look, ages ago, Debbie put on one of those classical but not too classical records — she must have been about ten or eleven, it was before she dyed her hair — and I said to you, 'That's that bloody tune they were driving me mad with when I was trying to write "Jean-Paul is up the Wall" in that hotel in Switzerland.' Maybe *she'll* remember.

CHARLOTTE.   Where is she? *(She has placed the record on the machine, which now starts to play the Skater's Waltz.)*

HENRY.   Riding stables. That's it! *(Triumphant and pleased, examining the record sleeve.) Skater's Waltz!* How did you know?

CHARLOTTE.   They don't have open-air dance floors in the Alps in mid-winter. They have skating rinks. Now you've got six.

HENRY.   Oh, I can't use that. It's too banal.

(The doorbell rings.)

HENRY.   *(Goes to take the record off the machine.)* That's Max. Do you want to let him in?

CHARLOTTE.   No. Say I'm not here.

HENRY.   He knows perfectly well you're here. Where else would you be? I'll say you don't want to see him because you've seen quite enough of him. How's that?

CHARLOTTE.   *(giving up)* Oh, I'll get dressed. *(She goes out the way she came in, towards the bedroom.)*

HENRY.   *(Goes out through another door into the hall. His voice and MAX's voice are heard, and the two men come in immediately afterwards.)* Hello, Max. Come in.

MAX.   Hello, Henry.

HENRY.   *(entering)* It's been some time.

MAX. *(enters unassertively)* Well, you've rather been keeping out of the way, haven't you?

HENRY. Yes. I'm sorry, Max. *(indicating the bedroom)* Charlotte's not here. How are you?

MAX. I'm all right.

HENRY. Good.

MAX. And you?

HENRY. I'm all right.

MAX. Good.

HENRY. Well, we all seem to be all right.

MAX. Is Charlotte all right?

HENRY. I don't think she's terribly happy. Well, is it coffee or open a bottle?

MAX. Bottle, I should think.

HENRY. Hang on, then. *(He goes out through the door to the kitchen. MAX turns aside and looks at a paper without interest.)*

(CHARLOTTE enters from the bedroom, having dressed without trying hard. She regards MAX, who then notices her.)

MAX. Hello, darling.

CHARLOTTE. Don't I get a day off?

MAX. *(apologetically)* Henry phoned...

CHARLOTTE. *(more kindly)* It's all right, Max.

HENRY. *(Enters busily from the kitchen, carrying an open champagne bottle and a jug of orange juice. Wine glasses are available in the living-room. HENRY puts himself in charge of arranging the drinks.)* Hello, Charlotte. I was just telling Max you weren't here. So nice to see you, Max. What are you doing with yourself?

MAX. Is he joking?

HENRY. I mean apart from that. Actors are so sensitive. They feel neglected if one isn't constantly going round to the theatre to check up on them.

MAX. I was just telling Henry off for keeping out of the way.

CHARLOTTE. You'd keep out of the way if you'd written it. *(To HENRY)* If that orange juice is for me, you can forget it.

HENRY. No, no — buck's fizz all round. I feel reckless, extravagant, famous, in love, and I'm next week's castaway on *Desert Island Discs.*

MAX. Are you really?

HENRY. Head over heels. Here you are, lover. How was last night, by the way? *(He hands MAX and CHARLOTTE their glasses.)*

CHARLOTTE. Hopeless. I had to fake it again.

HENRY. Very witty woman, my present wife. Actually, I was talking about my play.

CHARLOTTE. Actually, so was I. I've decided it's a mistake appearing in Henry's play.

MAX. Not for me, it isn't.

CHARLOTTE. Well, of course not for you, you idiot, you're not his wife.

MAX. Oh, I see what you mean.

CHARLOTTE. Max sees what I mean. You're right, Max.

MAX. I never said anything!

HENRY. How was it really? — last night.

CHARLOTTE. Not good. The stalls had a deserted look, about two-thirds, I should think. *(with false innocence)* Oh, sorry, darling, is that what you meant?

MAX. *(disapproving)* Honestly, Charlotte. It was all right, Henry, *really.* All the laughs were in place, for a Saturday night anyway, and I had someone who came round afterwards who said the reconciliation scene was extremely moving. Actually, that reminds me. They *did* say — I mean, it's a tiny thing but I thought I'd pass it on because I do feel rather the same way ... I mean all that stuff about the Japanese and digital watches — they suddenly have no idea what I'm talking about, you see, and I thought if we could just try it one night without—

HENRY. *(Halts him, like a traffic policeman.)* Excuse me, Max. *(He turns to CHARLOTTE.)* Two-thirds empty or two-thirds full?

CHARLOTTE. *(Laughs brazenly.)* Hard luck, Max. *(She toasts.)* Well, here's to closing night. To the collapse of *House of Cards.*

MAX. *(shocked)* Charlotte!

CHARLOTTE. Well, you try playing the feed one night instead of acting Henry after a buck's fizz and two re-writes. All *his* laughs are in place all right. So's my groan. Groan, groan, they all go when they find out. Oh, *groan,* so she hasn't got a lover at all, eh? And they lose interest in me totally. I'm a victim of Henry's fantasy — a quiet, faithful bird with an interesting job, and a recipe drawer, and a stiff upper lip — 'I'm sorry if you've had a bad time ... There's a right thing to say now...'

MAX. Jesus, Charlotte—

CHARLOTTE. *(quite genially)* Oh, shut up, Max. If he'd given her a lover instead of a temporary passport, we'd be in a play.

HENRY. It's a little early in the day for all this.

CHARLOTTE. No, darling, it's a little late.

MAX. Er, where's young Deborah today?

CHARLOTTE. Who?

MAX. Debbie.

CHARLOTTE. *(baffled)* Debbie?

MAX. Your daughter.

CHARLOTTE. Oh, daughter.

HENRY. Riding school.

CHARLOTTE. Must be some mistake. Smart talk, that's the thing. Having children is so unsmart. Endless dialogue about acne. Henry couldn't do that. He doesn't like research.

HENRY. True.

MAX. *(to CHARLOTTE)* Lots of people don't have children, in real life. Me and Annie...

HENRY. Oh, don't— I told her once that lots of women were only good for fetching drinks, and she became quite unreasonable. *(Blithely, knowing what he is doing, He holds his empty glass towards CHARLOTTE.)* Is there any more of that?

MAX. *(Glances at CHARLOTTE and hastily tries to defuse the bomb.)* Let me... *(He takes HENRY's glass and fills it from the bottle and the jug.)*

CHARLOTTE. Lots of *men* are only good for fetching drinks — why don't you write about *them?* *(MAX hands the glass back to HENRY.)*

HENRY. *(smiling up at MAX)* Terribly pleased you could come round.

CHARLOTTE. Oh, yes, you owe him a drink. What an

ego trip! Having all the words to come back with just as
you need them. That's the difference between plays and
real life — thinking time. You don't really think that if
Henry caught me out with a lover, he'd sit around being
witty about Rembrandt place mats? Like hell he would.
He'd come apart like a pick-a-sticks. His sentence struc-
ture would go to pot, closely followed by his sphincter.
You know that, don't you, Henry? Henry? No answer.
Are you there, Henry? Say something witty.

HENRY. *(Turns his head to her.)* Is it anyone I know?

MAX. *(starting to rise)* Well, look, thanks for the
drink—

CHARLOTTE. Oh, sit down, Max, for God's sake, or
he'll think it's you.

HENRY. It isn't you, is it, Max?

MAX. Oh, for Christ's sake... *(He subsides unhappily.)*

HENRY. Just kidding, Max. Badinage. You know,
dialogue.

(The doorbell rings.)

HENRY. See what I mean?

MAX. Annie said she'd come round if her committee
finished early. She's on this Justice for Brodie Committee
... you know... *(pause)* I'll go, should I?

HENRY. I'll go.

MAX. No, stay where you are, I'll see if it's her. *(He goes
out to the front door.)*

CHARLOTTE. Thanks very much. Anyone else coming?

HENRY. Just give them a cheese stick. They won't
stay.

CHARLOTTE. What did you phone him for in the first place?

HENRY. Well, I only have to write it once. He has to show up every night. I had a conscience.

CHARLOTTE. Do you have a conscience about me too?

HENRY. Absolutely. You can have a cheese stick.

CHARLOTTE. Well, don't ask her about Brodie.

HENRY. Right.

CHARLOTTE. If she starts on about scapegoats and cover-ups, she'll get a cheese stick up her nostril.

HENRY. Right.

CHARLOTTE. *(enthusiastically)* Darling! It's been ages!

(ANNIE has entered, followed by MAX. ANNIE is carrying a carrier bag loaded with greengrocery.)

ANNIE. Hello, Charlotte. This is jolly nice of you.

MAX. We can only stay a minute.

ANNIE. How are you, Henry?

HENRY. Fine.

MAX. Annie's stewarding at the protest meeting this afternoon, so we can't—

HENRY. Oh, do shut up. Don't take any notice of Max. I made him nervous.

ANNIE. What did you do to him?

HENRY. Nothing at all. I asked him if he was having an affair with Charlotte, and he was offended.

ANNIE. Was he?

HENRY. Apparently not. Been shopping?

ANNIE. Not exactly. I saw a place open on my way back

and... Anyway, you might as well take it as an offering.

CHARLOTTE. *(taking the bag from her and investigating it)* Darling, there was absolutely no need to bring ... mushrooms?

ANNIE. Yes.

CHARLOTTE. *(not quite behaving well)* And a turnip...

ANNIE. *(getting unhappy)* And carrots... Oh, dear, it must look as if—

HENRY. Where's the meat?

CHARLOTTE. Shut up.

ANNIE. I wish I'd brought flowers now.

CHARLOTTE. This is much nicer.

HENRY. So original. I'll get a vase.

ANNIE. It's supposed to be crudités.

HENRY. Crudités!

CHARLOTTE. I'll make a dip.

MAX. We're not staying to eat, for heaven's sake.

HENRY. Just a quick dip.

ANNIE. Would you like *me* to?

CHARLOTTE. No, no. I know where everything is.

HENRY. Yes, Charlotte will provide dips for the crudity. She knows where everything is. *(CHARLOTTE takes charge of the vegetables. HENRY gets a fourth glass.)* Sit down, have some buck's fizz. I feel reckless, extravagant, famous, and I'm next week's castaway on *Desert Island Discs.* You can be my luxury if you like.

ANNIE. I'm not sure I'm one you can afford.

MAX. What are your eight records?

HENRY. This is the problem. I hate music.

CHARLOTTE. He likes pop music.

HENRY. You don't have to repeat everything I say.

MAX. I don't understand the problem.

CHARLOTTE. The problem is he's a snob without being an inverted snob. He's *ashamed* of liking pop music. *(CHARLOTTE takes the vegetables out into the kitchen, closing the door.)*

HENRY. This is true. The trouble is I don't like the pop music which it's all right to like. You can have a bit of Pink Floyd shoved in between your symphonies and your Dame Janet Baker — that shows a refreshing breadth of taste or at least a refreshing candour — but *I* like Wayne Fontana and the Mindbenders doing 'Um Um Um Um Um Um'.

MAX. Doing what?

HENRY. That's the title. *(He demonstrates it.)* 'Um-Um-Um-Um-Um-Um'. I like Neil Sedaka. Do you remember 'Oh, Carol'?

MAX. For God's sake.

HENRY. *(cheerfully)* Yes, I'm not very up to date. I like Herman's Hermits, and the Hollies, and the Everly Brothers, and Brenda Lee, and the Supremes ... I don't mean everything they did. I don't like *artists*. I like singles.

MAX. This is sheer pretension.

HENRY. *(insistently)* No. It *moves* me, the way people are supposed to be moved by *real* music. I was taken once to Covent Garden to hear a woman called Callas in a sort of foreign musical with no dancing which people were donating kidneys to get tickets for. The idea was that I would be cured of my strange disability. As though the

place were a kind of Lourdes for the musically disadvan-
taged. My illness at the time took the form of believing
that the Righteous Brothers' recording of 'You've Lost
that Lovin' Feelin' ' on the London label was possibly the
most haunting, the most deeply moving noise ever produced by the human spirit, and this female vocalist person was going to set me right.

MAX. No good?

HENRY. Not even close. That woman would have had a
job getting into the top thirty if she were *hyped.*

MAX. You preferred the Brothers.

HENRY. I did. Do you think there's something wrong
with me?

MAX. Yes. I'd say you were a moron.

HENRY. What can I do?

MAX. There's nothing you can do.

HENRY. I mean about *Desert Island Discs.*

ANNIE. You know damned well what you should
do.

HENRY. Cancel?

MAX. Actually, I remember it. *(He sings, badly.)*
You've lost that lovin' feeling...

HENRY. That's an idea — aversion therapy.

MAX. *(Sings.)*
... That lovin' feeling ... You've lost that lovin'
feeling...

HENRY. I think it's working.

MAX. *(Sings.)*
It's gorn, gorn, gorn ... oh-oh-oh-yeah...

HENRY. *(happily)* God, it's *rubbish!* You've cracked it.
Now do 'Oh Carol'.

MAX. I don't know that one.

HENRY. I'll play it for you.

MAX. I think I'll go and help Charlotte.

ANNIE. I should go.

MAX. No. I thought of it first.

(CHARLOTTE enters, carrying a bowl.)

CHARLOTTE. One dip.

MAX. I was coming to help.

CHARLOTTE. All right, you can chop.

MAX. Fine. Chop... *(MAX goes out into the kitchen. CHARLOTTE places the bowl and is about to follow MAX out.)*

HENRY. *(Dips his finger into the bowl and tastes the dip.)* It needs something.

CHARLOTTE. I beg your pardon?

HENRY. It needs something. A bit of interest. Garlic? Lemon juice? I don't know.

CHARLOTTE. *(coldly)* Perhaps you should employ a cook.

HENRY. Surely that would be excessive — a cook who spends all her time emptying jars of mayonnaise and adding lemon juice? What would we do with the surplus?

CHARLOTTE. Presumably put it on stage with the rest of your stuff. *(She goes out into the kitchen, closing the door.)*

HENRY. *(pause)* Are you all right?

ANNIE. *(nods)* Are you all right? *(HENRY nods.)* Touch me. *(HENRY shakes his head.)* Touch me.

HENRY. No.

ANNIE. Come on, touch me. Help yourself. Touch me anywhere you like.

HENRY. No.

ANNIE. Touch me.

HENRY. No.

ANNIE. Coward.

HENRY. I love you anyway.

ANNIE. Yes, say that.

HENRY. I love you.

ANNIE. Go on.

HENRY. I love you.

ANNIE. That's it.

HENRY. I love you.

ANNIE. Touch me then. They'll come in or they won't. Take a chance. Kiss me.

HENRY. For Christ's sake.

ANNIE. Quick one on the carpet then.

HENRY. You're crackers.

ANNIE. I'm not interested in your mind.

HENRY. Yes, you are.

ANNIE. No, I'm not, I lied to you. *(Pause. HENRY smiles at her.)* I hate Sunday.

HENRY. Thought I'd cheer you up with an obscene phone call, but Max got to it first, so I improvised.

ANNIE. I might have come around anyway. 'Hello, Henry, Charlotte, just passing, long time no see.'

HENRY. That would have been pushing it.

ANNIE. I'm in a mood to push it. Let's go while they're chopping turnips.

HENRY. You *are* crackers.

ANNIE. We'll go, and then it will be done. Max will

suffer. Charlotte will make you suffer and get custody. You'll see Debbie on Sundays, and in three years she'll be at university not giving a damn either way.

HENRY. It's not just Debbie.

ANNIE. No, you want to give it time—

HENRY. Yes—

ANNIE. ...time to go wrong, change, spoil. Then you'll know it wasn't the real thing.

HENRY. I don't steal other men's wives.

ANNIE. Thanks a lot.

HENRY. You know what I mean.

ANNIE. Yes, you mean you love me but you don't want it to get around. Me and the Righteous Brothers. Well, thanks a lot.

(The kitchen door is flung open and MAX enters rather dramatically, bleeding from a cut finger.)

MAX. Don't panic! Have you got a hankie?

ANNIE. Max? *(ANNIE and HENRY respond appropriately, each searching for a handkerchief.)*

HENRY. *(Produces one first, a clean white one, from his pocket.)* Here—

MAX. Thanks. No, let me—

ANNIE. Let me see.

MAX. It's all right, it's not as bad as it looks. *(to HENRY)* Typical of your bloody kitchen — all champagne and no paper towels.

ANNIE. Poor love, just hold the cut for a while.

MAX. I think I'll put it back under the tap. *(He moves*

towards the kitchen.)

HENRY. Sorry about this, Max. She tried to do it to me once. *(MAX leaves.)*

ANNIE. I'm sorry.

HENRY. No, I'm sorry.

ANNIE. It's all right. Anything's all right.

HENRY. *(Moves forward and kisses her lightly.)* It'll get better.

ANNIE. How?

HENRY. Maybe we'll get found out.

ANNIE. Better to tell them. Whoever comes in first, eh? If it's Max, I'll tell him. If it's Charlotte, you start. All right? It's easy. Like Butch Cassidy and the Sundance Kid jumping off the cliff. It's only a couple of marriages and a child. All right?

(CHARLOTTE enters from the kitchen, carrying a tray of chopped-up vegetables.)

ANNIE. *(to HENRY)* All right? *(This is bold as brass and consequently, safe as houses: in this way ANNIE and HENRY continue to speak quite privately to each other in the interstices of the general conversation, under or over the respective preoccupations of CHARLOTTE and MAX.)*

CHARLOTTE. Did Max tell you? It's red cabbage. I've taken him off the knives. He's making another dip. He says it's Hawaiian. It's supposed to be served in an empty pineapple. We haven't got a pineapple. He's going to serve it in an empty tin of pineapple chunks. I do envy you being married to a man with a sense of humour.

Henry thinks he has a sense of humour, but what he has is a joke reflex. Eh, Henry? His mind is racing. Pineapple, pineapple... Come on, darling.

HENRY. *(to ANNIE)* No. Sorry.

ANNIE. It's all right.

CHARLOTTE. *(busy with cutlery)* Is Debbie expecting lunch?

HENRY. *(to ANNIE)* Not really.

CHARLOTTE. What?

HENRY. No. She wants to stay out.

ANNIE. *(Drinks what remains in her glass.)* Where is Debbie?

HENRY. Riding school. Drink? *(He takes her empty glass out of her hand.)*

ANNIE. Love you.

CHARLOTTE. She used to eat like a horse, till she had one.

HENRY. *(Refills ANNIE's glass.)* I'm picking her up this afternoon. *(He returns ANNIE's glass.)* Buck's fizz all right?

CHARLOTTE. Picking her up?

ANNIE. I don't care.

(MAX enters with the Hawaiian dip in the pineapple tin.)

MAX. Here we are.

ANNIE. Anything's all right.

MAX. It's Hawaiian.

HENRY. You're a lovely feller.

CHARLOTTE. Well done, Max.

ANNIE. So are you. *(She meets MAX, dips her finger into the tin and tastes the dip.)*

MAX. I hope I've got it right. What do you think? *(In his other hand MAX has HENRY's somewhat blood-stained handkerchief, which he now offers back. To HENRY.)* Thanks. What should I do with it?

HENRY. *(taking it)* It's okay, I'll take it. *(He puts the handkerchief in his pocket.)*

ANNIE. *(to MAX)* Not bad. *(to CHARLOTTE)* May I?

CHARLOTTE. Feel free.

ANNIE. Hang on a sec. *(She takes the tin from MAX and leaves the room with it, going to the kitchen.)*

CHARLOTTE. *(to HENRY)* You're over-protective. She could walk it in half an hour.

MAX. Who, what?

CHARLOTTE. Debbie.

HENRY. By the time she finished mucking out, whatever they call it...

CHARLOTTE. Grooming the mount, mounting the groom...

HENRY. *(unamused)* Hilarious.

MAX. I wouldn't let her walk. Someone got murdered on the common not long ago. Mustn't put temptation in the way.

CHARLOTTE. Debbie wouldn't murder anyone. She'd just duff them up a little bit. I can't make her out at all.

(ANNIE re-enters with the dip.)

CHARLOTTE. Some people have daughters who love ponies. *(Passing HENRY, ANNIE casually puts her finger in his mouth, without pausing.)*

ANNIE. What do you think?

CHARLOTTE. Some people have daughters who go punk. We've got one who goes riding on Barnes Common looking like the Last of the Mohicans.

HENRY. Crackers. *(ANNIE delivers the dip to CHARLOTTE.)*

CHARLOTTE. *(to ANNIE)* Is yours a case of sperm count or twisted tubes? Or is it that you just can't stand the little buggers?

MAX. Charlotte!

HENRY. What business is that of yours?

CHARLOTTE. He's in love with his, you know.

ANNIE. Isn't that supposed to be normal?

CHARLOTTE. No, dear, normal is the other way round.

HENRY. I say, Annie, what's this Brodie Committee all about? Charlotte was asking.

MAX. You know, Private Brodie.

ANNIE. It's all right.

MAX. Annie knows him.

ANNIE. I don't know him.

MAX. Tell them about meeting him on the train.

ANNIE. Yes, I met him on a train.

HENRY. *(Pause. Exhibiting avid interest, disobliges her.)* Yes?

ANNIE. *(laughs, uncomfortably.)* I seem to have told this story before.

HENRY. But we haven't seen you for ages.

MAX. Annie was travelling up to London from our cottage, weren't you?

HENRY. *Were* you?

ANNIE. Yes.

HENRY. *(fascinated)* You have a cottage in...?

ANNIE. Norfolk.

HENRY. Norfolk! What, up in the hills there?

ANNIE. *(testily) What* hills? Norfolk is absolutely— *(She brings herself up short.)*

CHARLOTTE. Oh, very funny. Stop it, Henry.

HENRY. I have no idea what you are talking about. So, you were coming up to London from your Norfolk flat— *cottage* — and you met this Private Brodie on the train.

ANNIE. Yes.

MAX. It was quite remarkable. Brodie was on his way to the anti-missiles demonstration, just like Annie.

HENRY. *Really?*

ANNIE. Yes.

HENRY. How did you know? Was he wearing a 'Missiles Out' badge on his uniform?

ANNIE. He wasn't in uniform.

MAX. The guts of it, the sheer moral courage. An ordinary soldier using his weekend pass to demonstrate against their bloody missiles.

HENRY. *Their?* I thought they were ours.

MAX. No, they're American.

HENRY. Oh, yes — *their...*

MAX. Pure moral conscience, you see — I mean, he didn't have our motivation.

HENRY. *Our?*

MAX. Mine and Annie's. *(HENRY appears not to understand.)* Owning property in Little Barmouth.

HENRY. Yes, of course. Private Brodie didn't own a

weekend cottage in Little Barmouth, you mean.

MAX. No, he's a Scots lad. He was stationed at the camp down the road. He was practically guarding the base where these rockets are making Little Barmouth into a sitting duck for the Russian counter-attack, should it ever come to that.

HENRY. *(to ANNIE)* I see what you mean.

ANNIE. Do you?

HENRY. Well, yes. Little Barmouth isn't going to declare war on Russia, so why should Little Barmouth be wiped out in a war not of Little Barmouth's making?

MAX. Quite.

CHARLOTTE. Shut up, Henry.

MAX. Is he being like that?

CHARLOTTE. Yes, he's being like that.

MAX. I don't see what he's got to be like that about.

HENRY. *(capitulating enthusiastically)* Absolutely! So you met his Private Brodie on the train, and Brodie said, 'I see you're going to the demo down Whitehall.' Right?

ANNIE. No. He recognized me from my children's serial. He used to watch *Rosie of the Royal Infirmary* when he was a kid.

MAX. How *about* that? It seems like the day before yesterday Annie was doing *Rosie of the Royal Infirmary.* He's *still* a kid.

ANNIE. Yes. Twenty-one.

MAX. He's a child.

HENRY. He kicked two policemen inside out, didn't he?

MAX. Piss off. *(to CHARLOTTE)* If you want to know what it's all about, you should come to the meeting.

CHARLOTTE. I know I should, but I like to keep my Sundays free. For entertaining friends, I mean. Fortunately, there are people like Annie to make up for people like me.

HENRY. Perhaps I'll go.

CHARLOTTE. No, you're people like me. You tell him, Annie.

ANNIE. You're picking up Debbie from riding school.

HENRY. Actually, I think I'll join the Justice for Brodie Committee. I should have thought of that before.

CHARLOTTE. They don't want dilettantes. You have to be properly motivated, like Annie.

HENRY. Brodie just wants to get out of jail. What does he care if we're motivated by the wrong reasons.

MAX. Like what?

HENRY. Perhaps one of us is worried that his image is getting a bit too right-of-centre. Another is in love with a committee member and wishes to gain her approbation...

CHARLOTTE. Which one are you?

HENRY. You think I'm kidding, but I'm not. Public postures have the configuration of private derangement.

MAX. Who said that?

HENRY. I did, you fool.

MAX. I mean first.

HENRY. Oh, first. *(to ANNIE)* Take him off to your meeting, I'm sick of him.

ANNIE. He's not coming.

HENRY. *(savouring it)* You are not going to the

meeting?

MAX. No, actually. Not that I wouldn't, but it would mean letting down my squash partner.

HENRY. Squash partner? An interesting moral dilemma. I wonder what Saint Augustine would have done?

MAX. I don't think Saint Augustine had a squash partner.

HENRY. I know that. Nobody would play with him. Even so. I put myself in his place. I balance a pineapple chunk on my carrot. I ponder. On the one hand, Max's squash partner. Decent chap but not a deprivation of the first magnitude. And on the other hand, Brodie, an out-and-out thug, an arsonist, vandalizer of a national shrine, *but* mouldering in jail for years to come owing, *perhaps*, to society's inability to comprehend a man divided against himself, a pacifist Hooligan.

MAX. I don't condone vandalism, however idealistic. I just—

HENRY. Yes, well, as acts of vandalism go, starting a fire on a war memorial using the wreath to the Unknown Soldier as kindling scores very low on discretion. I assumed he was trying to be provocative.

MAX. Of course he was, you idiot. But he got hammered by an emotional backlash.

HENRY. No, no, you *can't*—

MAX. Yes, he bloody was!

HENRY. I mean 'hammer' and 'backlash'. You can't *do it!*

MAX. Oh, for Christ's sake. This is your house, and I'm drinking your wine, but if you don't mind me saying so, Henry—

HENRY. *My* saying, Max.

MAX. Right. *(He puts down his glass definitively and stands up.)* Come on, Annie. There's something wrong with you. You've got something missing. You may have all the words, but having all the words is not what life's about.

HENRY. I'm sorry, but it actually *hurts.*

MAX. Brodie may be no intellectual, like you, but he did march for a cause, and now he's got six years for a stupid piece of bravado and a punch-up, and he'd have been forgotten in a week if it wasn't for Annie. That's what life's about — messy bits of good and bad luck, and people caring and not necessarily having all the answers. Who the hell are you to patronize Annie? She's worth ten of you.

HENRY. I know that.

MAX. I'm sorry, Charlotte.

CHARLOTTE. Well done, Henry. *(MAX leaves towards the front door. CHARLOTTE, with a glance at HENRY, rolling her eyes in rebuke, follows him out of the room. ANNIE stands up. For the rest of the scene she is moving, hardly looking at HENRY, perhaps fetching her handbag.)*

HENRY. It was just so I could look at you without it looking funny.

ANNIE. What time are you going for Debbie?

HENRY. Four o'clock. Why?

ANNIE. Three o'clock. Look for my car.

HENRY. What about Brodie?

ANNIE. Let him rot. *(She leaves, closing the door.)*

(Pop music: Herman's Hermits, 'I'm Into Something Good'.)

Scene Three

A living-room. MAX is alone, listening to a small radio, from which Herman's Hermits continue to be heard, at an adjusted level. The disposition of furniture and doors makes the scene immediately reminiscent of the beginning of Scene One. The front door, off stage, is heard opening with a key. The door closes. ANNIE, wearing a topcoat, appears briefly round the door to the hall. She is in a hurry.

ANNIE. Have you got it on? *(She disappears and reappears without the coat.)* How much have I missed?

MAX. Five or ten minutes.

ANNIE. Damn. If I'd had the car, I'd have caught the beginning.

MAX. Where have you been?

ANNIE. You know where I've been. Rehearsing.

(The music ends and is followed by HENRY being interviewed on Desert Island Discs, *but the radio dialogue, during the few moments before MAX turns the sound down, is meaningless under the stage dialogue.)*

MAX. How's Julie?

ANNIE. Who?

MAX. Julie. Miss Julie. Strindberg's Miss Julie. Miss Julie by August Strindberg, how is she?

ANNIE. Are you all right?

MAX. This probably—

ANNIE. Shush up.

MAX. This probably isn't anything, but—

ANNIE. *Max, can I listen? (MAX turns the radio sound right down.)* What's up? Are you cross?

MAX. This probably isn't anything, but I found this in the car, between the front seats. *(He shows her a soiled and blood-stained white handkerchief.)*

ANNIE. What is it?

MAX. Henry's handkerchief.

ANNIE. Well, give it back to him. *(She reaches for it.)* Here, I'll wash it and you can give it to Charlotte at the theatre.

MAX. I did give it back to him. When was he in the car? *(pause)* It was a clean handkerchief, apart from my blood. Have you got a cold? It looks filthy. It's dried filthy. You're filthy. You filthy cow. You rotten filthy—*(He starts to cry, barely audible, immobile. ANNIE waits. He recovers his voice.)* It's not true, is it?

ANNIE. Yes.

MAX. Oh, God. *(He stands up.)* Why did you?

ANNIE. I'm awfully sorry, Max—

MAX. *(interrupting, suddenly pulled together)* All right. It happened. All right. It didn't mean anything.

ANNIE. I'm awfully sorry, Max, but I love him.

MAX. Oh, no.

ANNIE. Yes.

MAX. Oh, *no.* You don't.

ANNIE. Yes, I do. And he loves me. That's that, isn't it? I'm sorry it's awful. But it's better really. All that lying.

MAX. *(breaking up again)* Oh, Christ, Annie, stop it. I love you. Please don't—

ANNIE. Come on, please — it doesn't have to be like this.

MAX. How long for? And *him* — oh, *God. (He kicks the radio savagely.)*

(The radio has gone into music again — the Righteous Brothers singing 'You've Lost That Lovin' Feelin' ' — and MAX's kick has the effect of turning up the volume rather loud. He flings himself upon ANNIE in something like an assault which turns immediately into an embrace. ANNIE does no more than suffer the embrace, looking over MAX's shoulder, her face blank.)

Scene Four

Living-room. Obviously temporary and makeshift quarters, divided Left and Right by a clothes rail, making two areas, 'his' and 'hers'. HENRY is alone, writing at a desk. On the floor are a number of cardboard boxes containing files, papers, letters, scripts, bills... The pillage of a filing system. There is also a couch. The Sunday newspapers and a bound script are on or near the couch. A radio plays pop music quietly while HENRY writes. ANNIE enters from the bedroom door, barefoot and wearing HENRY's robe, which is too big for her. HENRY, in mid-sentence, looks up briefly and looks down again.

ANNIE. I'm not here. Promise. *(She goes to the couch and carefully opens a newspaper. HENRY continues to write. ANNIE glances towards him once or twice. He takes no notice. She stands up and goes behind his chair, looking over his shoulder as he works. He takes no notice. She goes round the desk and stands in front of him. He takes no notice. She flashes open the robe for his benefit. He takes no notice. She moves round behind him again and looks over his shoulder.)*

HENRY. *(He turns and grabs her with great suddenness, causing her to scream and laugh. The assault turns into a standing embrace.)* You're a bloody nuisance.

ANNIE. Sorry, sorry, sorry. I'll be good. I'll sit and learn my script.

HENRY. No you won't.

ANNIE. I'll go in the other room.

HENRY. This room will do.

ANNIE. No, you've got to do my play.

HENRY. I can't write it. Let me off.

ANNIE. No, you promised. It's my gift.

HENRY. All right. Stay and talk a minute. *(He turns off the radio.)* Raw material, then I'll do this page, then I'll rape you, then I'll do the page again, then I'll — Oh *(happily)*, are you all right?

ANNIE. *(nods)* Yeah. Are you all right? *(He nods. Gleefully, self-reproachful.)* Isn't it awful? Max is so unhappy while I feel so ... *thrilled.* His misery just seems ... not in very good taste. Am I awful? He leaves letters for me at rehearsal, you know, and gets me to come to the phone by pretending to be my agent and people. He loves me, and he wants to punish me with his pain, but I can't come up with the proper guilt. I'm sort of irritated by it. It's so *tiring* and so *uninteresting.* You never write about that, you lot.

HENRY. What?

ANNIE. Gallons of ink and miles of typewriter ribbon expended on the misery of the unrequited lover; not a word about the utter tedium of the unrequiting. It's a very interesting...

HENRY. Lacuna?

ANNIE. What? No, I mean it's a very interesting sort of...

HENRY. Prejudice?

ANNIE. It's a very interesting ... thing.

HENRY. Yes, thing.

ANNIE. No, I mean it shows — never mind — I've lost it now.

HENRY. How are you this morning?

ANNIE. One behind. Where were you?

HENRY. You were flat out.

ANNIE. Your own fault. When I take a sleeping pill, I'm on the downhill slope. You should have come to bed when you said.

HENRY. *(indicating his desk)* It wasn't where I could leave it. I would have gone to sleep depressed.

ANNIE. Well, I thought, the honeymoon is over. Fifteen days and fuckless to bye-byes.

HENRY. No, actually, I managed.

ANNIE. You did not.

HENRY. Yes, I did. You were totally zonked. Only your reflexes were working.

ANNIE. Liar.

HENRY. Honestly.

ANNIE. Why didn't you wake me?

HENRY. I thought I'd try it without you talking. Look, I'm not doing any good, why don't we—?

ANNIE. You rotter. Just for that I'm going to learn my script.

HENRY. I'll read in for you.

ANNIE. *(Glowers at him but finds a page in the script and hands the script to him.)* You didn't really, did you?

HENRY. Yes.

ANNIE. *(She 'reads' without inflection.)* 'Très gentil, Monsieur Jean, très gentil!'

HENRY. *(reading)* *'Vous voulez plaisanter, madame!'*

ANNIE. *'Et vous voulez parler francais?'* Where did you pick that up?'

HENRY. 'In Switzerland. I worked as a waiter in one of the best hotels in Lucerne.'

ANNIE. 'You're quite the gentleman in that coat... *charmant.'* You rotter.

HENRY. 'You flatter me, Miss Julie.'

ANNIE. 'Flatter? I flatter?'

HENRY. 'I'd like to accept the compliment, but modesty forbids. And, of course, my modesty entails your insincerity. Hence, you flatter me.'

ANNIE. 'Where did you learn to talk like that? Do you spend a lot of time at the theatre?'

HENRY. 'Oh yes. I get about, you know.'

ANNIE. Oh, Hen. Are you all right?

HENRY. Not really. I can't do mine. I don't know how to write love. I try to write it properly, and it just comes out embarrassing. It's either childish or it's rude. And the rude bits are absolutely juvenile. I can't use any of it. My credibility is already hanging by a thread after *Desert Island Discs.* Anyway, I'm too prudish. Perhaps I should write it completely artificial. Blank verse. Poetic imagery. Not so much of the 'Will you still love me when my tits are droopy?' 'Of course I will, darling, it's your bum I'm mad for', and more of the 'By my troth, thy beauty maketh the moon hide her radiance', do you think?

ANNIE. Not really, no.

HENRY. No. Not really. I don't know. Loving and being loved is unliterary. It's happiness expressed in banality and lust. It makes me nervous to see three-quarters of a page and no *writing* on it. I mean, I *talk* better than this.

ANNIE. You'll have to learn to do sub-text. My Strindberg is steaming with lust, but there is nothing rude on the page. We just talk round it. Then he sort of bites my finger and I do the heavy breathing and he gives me a quick feel, kisses me on the neck...

HENRY. Who does?

ANNIE. Gerald. It's all very exciting. *(HENRY laughs, immoderately, and ANNIE continues coldly.)* Or amusing, of course.

HENRY. We'll do that bit ... you breathe, I'll feel...

ANNIE. *(She pushes him away.)* Go away. You'll just get moody afterwards.

HENRY. When was I ever moody?

ANNIE. Whenever you get seduced from your work.

HENRY. You mean the other afternoon?

ANNIE. What other afternoon? No, I don't mean *seduced*, for God's sake. Can't you think about anything else?

HENRY. Certainly. Like what?

ANNIE. I mean 'seduced', like when you're seduced by someone on the television.

HENRY. I've never been seduced on the television.

ANNIE. You were seduced by Miranda Jessop on the television.

HENRY. Professional duty.

ANNIE. If she hadn't been in it, you wouldn't have watched that play if they'd come round and done it for you on your carpet.

HENRY. Exactly. I had a postcard from her agent,

would I be sure to watch her this week in *Trotsky Playhouse* or whatever they call it.

ANNIE. You only looked up when she stripped off. Think I can't see through you? That's why I took my pill. Screw you, I thought, feel free.

HENRY. You're daft. I've got to watch her if she's going to do my telly. It's just good manners.

ANNIE. *Her* tits are droopy already.

HENRY. I'm supposed to have an opinion, you see.

ANNIE. I think she's bloody overrated, as a matter of fact.

HENRY. I have to agree. I wouldn't give them more than six out of ten. *(She clouts him with her script.)* Four. *(She clouts him again.)* Three.

ANNIE. You think you're so bloody funny.

HENRY. What's up with you? I hardly know the woman.

ANNIE. You'll like her. She wears leopard-skin pants.

HENRY. How do you know?

ANNIE. I shared a dressing-room with her.

HENRY. I don't suppose she wears them all the time.

ANNIE. I'm bloody sure she doesn't.

HENRY. 'By my troth thy beauty maketh the moon—'

ANNIE. Oh, shut up.

HENRY. What are you jealous about?

ANNIE. I'm not jealous.

HENRY. All right, what are you cross about?

ANNIE. I'm not cross. Do your work. *(She makes a show of concentrating on her script.)*

HENRY. *(Makes a show of resuming work. Pause.)* I'm sorry.

ANNIE. What for?

HENRY. I don't know. I'll have to be going out to pick up Debbie. I don't want to go if we're not friends. Will you come, then?

ANNIE. No. It was a mistake last time. It spoils it for her, being nervous.

HENRY. She wasn't nervous.

ANNIE. Not her. You.

HENRY. *(pause)* Well, I'll be back around two.

ANNIE. I won't be here.

HENRY. *(pause, remembering)* Oh, yes. Is it today you're going prison-visiting? You're being very — um — faithful to Brodie.

ANNIE. That surprises you, does it?

HENRY. I only mean that you haven't got much time for good causes. You haven't got a weekend cottage either.

ANNIE. You think I'm more like you.

HENRY. Yes.

ANNIE. It's just that I happen to know him.

HENRY. You don't know him. You met him on a train.

ANNIE. Well, he's the only political prisoner I've ever met on train. He's lucky.

HENRY. Political?

ANNIE. It was a political act which got him jumped on by the police in the first place so it's...

HENRY. A priori?

ANNIE. No, it's—

HENRY. De facto?

ANNIE. It's common sense that resisting arrest isn't the same as a criminal doing it.

HENRY. Arson is a criminal offence.

ANNIE. Arson is burning down buildings. Setting fire to the wreath on the war memorial is a symbolic act. Surely you can see the difference?

HENRY. *(carefully)* Oh, yes... That's ... easy to see. *(not carefully enough)*

ANNIE. *(Looks at him narrowly.)* And, of course, he did get hammered by an emotional backlash.

HENRY. *(pause)* Do you mean real leopard skin or just printed nylon?

ANNIE. *(Erupts and assails him, shouting.)* You don't love me the way I love you. I'm just a relief after Charlotte, and a novelty.

HENRY. You're a novelty all right. I never *met* anyone so silly. I love you. I don't know why you're behaving like this.

ANNIE. I'm behaving normally. It's you who's abnormal. You don't care enough to *care.* Jealousy is normal.

HENRY. I thought you said you *weren't* jealous.

ANNIE. Well, why aren't *you* ever jealous?

HENRY. Of whom?

ANNIE. Of anybody. You don't care if Gerald Jones sticks his tongue in my ear — which, incidentally, he does whenever he gets the chance.

HENRY. Is that what this is all about?

ANNIE. It's insulting the way you just laugh.

HENRY. But you've got no interest in him.

ANNIE. I know that, but why should you assume it?

HENRY. Because you haven't. This is stupid.

ANNIE. But why don't you *mind?*

HENRY. I do.

ANNIE. No, you don't.

HENRY. That's true, I don't. Why is that? It's because I feel superior. There he is, poor bugger, picking up the odd crumb of ear wax from the rich man's table. You're right. I don't mind. I like it. I like the way his presumption admits his poverty. I like him, knowing that that's all there is, because you're coming home to me and we don't want anyone else. I love love. I love having a lover and being one. The insularity of passion. I love it. I love the way it blurs the distinction between everyone who isn't one's lover. Only two kinds of presence in the world. There's you and there's them. I love you so.

ANNIE. I love you so, Hen. *(They kiss.)*

(The alarm on HENRY's wristwatch goes off. They separate.)

HENRY. Sorry.

ANNIE. Don't get kicked by the horse.

HENRY. Don't get kicked by Brodie. *(He goes to the door to leave. At the door he looks at her and nods. She nods at him. He leaves. ANNIE goes slowly to HENRY's desk and looks at the pages on it. She turns on the radio and turns it from pop to Bach. She goes back to the desk and, almost absently, opens one of the drawers. Leaving it open, she goes to the door and disappears briefly into the hall, then reappears, closing the door. She goes to one of the cardboard boxes on the floor. She removes the contents from the box. She places the pile of papers on the floor. Squatting down, she starts going through the pile, methodically and unhurriedly. The radio plays on.)*

ACT TWO

Scene One

Living-room/study. Three doors. Two years later. A different house. The two years ought to show on HENRY and on ANNIE. Perhaps he now uses glasses when he is reading, as he is at the beginning of the scene, or he may even have grown a moustache. ANNIE may have cut her hair short. Opera (Verdi) is playing on the record player. There is a TV and video and a small radio on HENRY's desk, on which there is also a typewriter. HENRY is alone, reading a script which consists of a sheaf of typed pages. HENRY reads for a few moments. ANNIE enters from bedroom or kitchen and glances at HENRY, not casually, then sits down and watches him read for a moment. Then she looks away and listens to the music for a moment. HENRY glances up at her. ANNIE looks at him.

ANNIE. Well?
HENRY. Oh — um — Strauss.
ANNIE. What?
HENRY. Not Strauss.
ANNIE. I meant the play.
HENRY. *(indicating the script)* Ah. The play.

ANNIE. *(scornfully) Strauss.* How can it be Strauss? It's in Italian.

HENRY. Is it? *(He listens.)* So it is. Italian opera. One of the Italian operas. Verdi.

ANNIE. Which one?

HENRY. Giuseppe. *(He judges from her expression that this is not the right answer.)* Monty?

ANNIE. I mean which *opera.*

HENRY. Ah. *(confidently)* Madame Butterfly.

ANNIE. You're doing it on purpose. *(She goes to the record player and stops it playing.)*

HENRY. I promise you.

ANNIE. You'd think that *something* would have sunk in after two years and a bit.

HENRY. I like it — I really do like it — quite, it's just that I can't tell them apart. Two years and a bit isn't very long when they're all going for the same sound. Actually, I've got a better ear than you — *you* can't tell the difference between the Everly Brothers and the Andrews Sisters.

ANNIE. There isn't any difference.

HENRY. Or we could split up. Can we have something decent on now?

ANNIE. No.

HENRY. All right. Put on one of your instrumental numbers. The big band sound. *(He does the opening of Beethovan's Fifth.)* Da — da — da — *dah...*

ANNIE. Get *on.*

HENRY. Right. *(He turns his attention to the script.)* Stop me if anybody has said this before, but it's interesting how many of the all-time greats begin with B: Beethoven, the

Big Bopper...

ANNIE. That's all they have in common.

HENRY. I wouldn't say that. They're both dead. The Big Bopper died in the same plane crash that killed Buddy Holly and Richie Valens, you know.

ANNIE. No, I didn't know. Have you given up on the play or what?

HENRY. Buddy Holly was twenty-two. Think of what he might have gone on to achieve. I mean, if Beethoven had been killed in a plane crash at twenty-two, the history of music would have been very different. As would the history of aviation, of course.

ANNIE. *Henry.*

HENRY. The play. *(He turns his attention back to the script.)*

ANNIE. How far have you got?

HENRY. Do you have a professional interest in this or is it merely personal?

ANNIE. Merely?

HENRY. *(pause)* Do you have a personal interest in this or is it merely professional?

ANNIE. Which one are you dubious about?

HENRY. *(pause)* Pause.

ANNIE. I could do her, couldn't I?

HENRY. Mary? Oh, sure — without make-up.

ANNIE. Well, then. *Three Sisters* is definitely off.

HENRY. Nothing's definite with that lot.

ANNIE. The other two are pregnant.

HENRY. Half a dozen new lines could take care of that.

ANNIE. If this script could be in a fit state, say, a month

from now—

HENRY. Anyway, I thought you were committing incest in Glasgow.

ANNIE. I haven't said I'll do it.

HENRY. I think you should. It's classy stuff, Webster. I love all that Jacobean sex and violence.

ANNIE. It's Ford, not Webster. *And* it's Glasgow.

HENRY. Don't you work north of the West End, then?

ANNIE. I was thinking you might miss me — pardon my mistake.

HENRY. I was thinking you might like me to come with you — pardon mine.

ANNIE. You hadn't the faintest intention of coming to Glasgow for five weeks.

HENRY. That's true. I answered out of panic. Of course I'd miss you.

ANNIE. Also, it *is* somewhat north.

HENRY. *(He 'shoots' her between the eyes with his forefinger.)* Got you. Is it rehearsing in Glasgow?

ANNIE. *(nods)* After the first week. *(indicating the script)* Where've you got to?

HENRY. They're on the train. 'You're a strange boy, Billy. How old are you?' 'Twenty. But I've lived more than you'll ever live.' Should I read out loud?

ANNIE. If you like.

HENRY. Give you the feel of it.

ANNIE. All right.

HENRY. I'll go back a bit ... where they first meet. All right? *(ANNIE nods. HENRY makes train noises. She is defensive, not quite certain whether he is being wicked or not. He reads.)*

'Excuse me, is this seat taken?' 'No.' 'Mind if I sit down?'
'It's a free country.' 'Thank you.' He sits down opposite
her. MARY carries on with reading her book. 'Going far?'
'To London.' 'So, you were saying... So you think it's a
free country.' 'Don't you?' 'This is it, we're all free to do
as we're told. My name's Bill, by the way. What's yours?'
'Mary.' 'I'm glad to make your acquaintance, Mary.' 'I'm
glad to make yours, Bill.' 'Do you know what time this
train is due to arrive in London?' 'At about half-past one.
I believe, if it is on time.' 'You put me in mind of
Mussolini, Mary. Yes, you look just like him, you've got
the same eyes.'

ANNIE. If you're not going to read it properly, don't
bother.

HENRY. Sorry. 'At about half-past one, I believe, if it is
on time.' 'You put me in mind of Mussolini, Mary. People used to say about Mussolini, he may be a Fascist, but
at least the trains run on time. Makes you wonder why
British Rail isn't totally on time, eh?' 'What do you
mean?' 'I mean it's a funny thing. The Fascists are in
charge but the trains are late often as not.' 'But this isn't a
Fascist country.' 'Are you quite sure of that, Mary? Take
the army—' You're not going to do this, are you?

ANNIE. Why not?

HENRY. It's no good.

ANNIE. You mean it's not literary.

HENRY. It's not literary, and it's no good. He can't
write.

ANNIE. You're a snob.

HENRY. I'm a snob, and he can't write.

ANNIE. I know it's raw, but he's got something to
say.

HENRY. He's got something to say. It happens to be something extremely silly and bigoted. But leaving that aside, there is still the problem that he can't write. He can burn things down, but he can't write.

ANNIE. Give it back. I shouldn't have asked you.

HENRY. For God's sake, Annie, if it wasn't Brodie you'd never have got through it.

ANNIE. But it *is* Brodie. That's the point. Two and a half years ago he could hardly put six words together.

HENRY. He still can't.

ANNIE. You *pig*.

HENRY. I'm a pig, and he can't—

ANNIE. I'll smash you one. It's you who's bigoted. You're bigoted about what writing is supposed to be like. You judge everything as though everyone starts off from the same place, aiming at the same prize. English Lit. Shakespeare out in front by a mile, and the rest of the field strung out behind trying to close the gap. You all write for people who would like to write like you if only they could write. Well, screw you, and screw English Lit.!

HENRY. Right.

ANNIE. Brodie isn't writing to compete like you. He's writing to be heard.

HENRY. Right.

ANNIE. And he's done it on his own.

HENRY. Yes. Yes ... I can see he's done a lot of reading.

ANNIE. You can't expect it to be English Lit.

HENRY. No.

ANNIE. He's a prisoner shouting over the wall.

HENRY. Quite. Yes, I see what you mean.

ANNIE. Oh shut up! I'd rather have your sarcasm.

HENRY. Why a play? Did you suggest it?

ANNIE. Not exactly.

HENRY. Why did you?

ANNIE. The committee, what's left of it, thought ... I mean, people have got bored with Brodie. People get bored with anything after two or three years. The campaign needs...

HENRY. A shot in the arm?

ANNIE. No, it needs...

HENRY. A kick up the arse?

ANNIE. *(flares)* For Christ's sake, will you stop finishing my sentences for me!

HENRY. Sorry.

ANNIE. I've lost it now.

HENRY. The campaign needs...

ANNIE. A writer is harder to ignore. I thought, TV plays get talked about, make some impact. Get his case reopened. Do you think? I mean, Henry, what *do* you think?

HENRY. I think it makes a lot of sense.

ANNIE. No, what do you *really* think?

HENRY. Oh, *really* think. Well, I *really* think writing rotten plays is not in itself proof of rehabilitation. Still less of wrongful conviction. But even if it were, I think that anyone who thinks that they're bored with Brodie won't know what boredom is till they've sat through his apologia. Not that anyone will get the chance, because it's half as long as *Das Kapital* and only twice as funny. I also think you should know better.

ANNIE. You arrogant bastard.

HENRY. You swear too much.

ANNIE. Roger is willing to do it, in principle.

HENRY. What Roger? Oh *Roger*. Why the hell would Roger do it?

ANNIE. He's on the committee. *(HENRY looks at the ceiling.)* It just needs a bit of work.

HENRY. You're all bent.

ANNIE. You're jealous.

HENRY. Of Brodie?

ANNIE. You're jealous of the idea of the writer. You want to keep it sacred, special, not something anybody can do. Some of us have it, some of us don't. *We* write, *you* get written about. What gets you about Brodie is he doesn't know his place. You say he can't write like a head waiter saying you can't come in here without a tie. Because he can't put words together. What's so good about putting words together?

HENRY. It's traditionally considered advantageous for a writer.

ANNIE. He's not a writer. He's a convict. *You're* a writer. You write *because* you're a writer. Even when you write *about* something, you have to think up something to write about just so you can keep writing. More well chosen words nicely put together. So what? Why should that be *it?* Who says?

HENRY. Nobody says. It just works best.

ANNIE. Of *course* it works. You teach a lot of people what to expect from good writing, and you end up with a lot of people saying you write well. Then somebody who isn't in on the game comes along, like Brodie, who really has something to write about, something real, and you can't get through it. Well, *he* couldn't get through *yours*, so where are you? To you, he can't write. To him, write is all you *can* do.

HENRY. Jesus, Annie, you're beginning to appal me. There's something scary about stupidity made coherent. I can deal with idiots, and I can deal with sensible argument, but I don't know how to deal with you. Where's my cricket bat?

ANNIE. Your cricket bat?

HENRY. Yes. It's a new approach. *(He heads out into the hall.)*

ANNIE. Are you trying to be funny?

HENRY. No, I'm serious. *(He goes out while she watches in wary disbelief. He returns with an old cricket bat.)*

ANNIE. You better not be.

HENRY. Right, you silly cow—

ANNIE. Don't you bloody dare—

HENRY. Shut up and listen. This thing here, which looks like a wooden club, is actually several pieces of particular wood cunningly put together in a certain way so that the whole thing is sprung; like a dance floor. It's for hitting cricket balls with. If you get it right, the cricket ball will travel two hundred yards in four seconds, and all you've done is give it a knock like knocking the top off a bottle of stout, and it makes a noise like a trout taking a fly... *(He clucks his tongue to make the noise.)* What we're trying to do is to write cricket bats, so that when we throw up an idea and give it a little knock, it might ... *travel...(He clucks his tongue again and picks up the script.)* Now, what we've got here is a lump of wood of roughly the same shape trying to be a cricket bat, and if you hit a ball with it, the ball will travel about ten feet and you will drop the bat and dance about shouting 'Ouch!' with your hands stuck into your armpits. *(indicating the cricket bat)* This isn't better because someone says it's better, or because there's a conspiracy by the MCC to keep cudgels off the field. It's better because it's better. You don't believe me, so I suggest you go out to bat with this and see how you get on. 'You're a strange boy, Billy, how old are you?' 'Twenty, but I've lived more than you'll ever live.' Ooh, ouch! *(He drops the script and hops about with his hands in his armpits, going 'Ouch!')*

ANNIE. *(She watches him expressionlessly until he desists.)* I hate you.

HENRY. I love you. I'm your pal. I'm your best mate. I look after you. You're the only chap.

ANNIE. Oh, Hen... Can't you help?

HENRY. What did you expect me to do?

ANNIE. Well ... cut it and shape it...

HENRY. Cut it and shape it. Henry of Mayfair. Look — he can't write. I would have to write it for him.

ANNIE. Well, write it for him.

HENRY. I can't.

ANNIE. Why?

HENRY. Because it's *balls*. Announcing every stale revelation of the newly enlightened like stout Cortez coming upon the Pacific — war is profits, politicians are puppets, Parliament is a farce, justice is a fraud, property is theft... It's all here: pages and pages of it. It's like being run over very slowly by a traveling freak show of favourite simpletons, the india rubber pedagogue, the midget intellectual, the human panacea...

ANNIE. It's his view of the world. Perhaps from where he's standing you'd see it the same way.

HENRY. Or perhaps I'd realize where I'm standing. Or at least that I'm standing *somewhere*. There is, I suppose, a world of objects which have a certain form, like this coffee mug. I turn it, and it has no handle. I tilt it, and it has no cavity. But there is something real here which is always a mug with a handle. I suppose. But politics, justice, patriotism — they aren't even like coffee mugs. There's nothing real there separate from our perception of them. So if you try to change them as though there were something there to change, you'll get frustrated, and frustration will finally make you violent. If you know this and proceed with humility, you may perhaps alter people's perceptions so that they behave a little differently at that axis of behaviour where we locate politics or justice; but if you don't know this, then you're acting on a mistake. Prejudice is the expression of this mistake.

ANNIE. Or such is your perception.

HENRY. All right.

ANNIE. And who wrote it, why he wrote it, *where* he wrote it — none of these things count with you?

HENRY. Leave me out of it. They don't count. Maybe Brodie got a raw deal, maybe he didn't. I don't know. It doesn't count. He's a lout with language. I can't help somebody who thinks, or thinks he thinks, that editing a newspaper is censorship, or that throwing bricks is a demonstration while building tower blocks is social violence, or that unpalatable statement is provocation while disrupting the speaker is the exercise of free speech... Words don't deserve that kind of malarkey. They're innocent, neutral, precise, standing for this, describing that, meaning the other, so if you look after them you can build bridges across incomprehension and chaos. But when they get their corners knocked off, they're no good any more, and Brodie knocks their corners off. I don't think writers are sacred, but words are. They deserve respect. If you get the right ones in the right order, you can nudge the world a little or make a poem which children will speak for you when you're dead.

ANNIE. *(Goes to the typewriter, pulls out the page from the machine and reads it.)* 'Seventy-nine. Interior. Commander's capsule. From Zadok's p.o.v. we see the green glow of the laser strike-force turning towards us. BCU Zadok's grim smile. *Zadok:* "I think it's going to work. Here they come!" *Kronk,* voice over: "Hold your course!" *Zadok:* —'

HENRY. *(interrupts)* That's not words, that's pictures. The movies. Anyway, alimony doesn't count. If Charlotte made it legal with that architect she's shacked up with, I'd be writing the real stuff.

ANNIE. *(Lets the page drop onto the typewriter.)* You never wrote mine.

HENRY. That's true. I didn't. I tried. I can't remember when I last felt so depressed. Oh yes. Yesterday. Don't be rotten to me. I'll come to Glasgow and I'll sit in your dressing-room and I'll write Kronk and Zadok every night while you're doing *'Tis Pity She's a Whore.*

ANNIE. I'm not going to Glasgow.

HENRY. Yes, you bloody are.

ANNIE. No I'm bloody not. We'll get Brodie's play off

the ground. I want to do it. *I* want to do it. Don't *I* count? Hen? *(pause)* Well, I can see it's difficult for a man of your fastidious tastes. Let's have some literacy. Something decent. *(She stabs her finger onto the small radio on HENRY's desk.)*

(Quietly it starts playing pop. ANNIE starts to go out of the room.)

HENRY. *(exasperated) Why Brodie?* Do you fancy him or what? *(She looks back at him and he sees that he has made a mistake.)* I take it back.

ANNIE. Too late. *(She leaves the room.)*

Scene Two

ANNIE is sitting by the window of a moving train. She is immersed in a paperback book. BILLY walks into view and pauses, looking at her for a moment. She is unaware of his presence. He carries a zipped grip bag. He speaks with a Scottish accent.

BILLY. Excuse me, is this seat taken?

ANNIE. *(Hardly raises her eyes.)* No.

BILLY. *(Sits down next to or opposite her. He puts the grip on the seat next to him. He looks at her. She doesn't look up from her book. He looks at his watch and then out of the window and then back at her.)* You'd think with all these Fascists the trains would be on time.

ANNIE. *(Looks up at him and jumps a mile. She gives a little squeal.)* Jesus, you gave me a shock. *(She looks at him, pleased and amused.)* You fool.

BILLY. *(Drops the accent.)* Hello.

ANNIE. I didn't know you were on the train.

BILLY. Yes, well, there you are. How are you?

ANNIE. All right. I gather you read it, then.

BILLY. Brodie's play? Yes, I read it.

ANNIE. And?

BILLY. He can't write.

ANNIE. *(small pause)* I know. I just thought it was some-

65

thing you'd do well.

BILLY.   Oh, yes. I could do a job on it. Are you going to do it?

ANNIE.   I hope so. Not as it is, I suppose. Thank you for reading it anyway.

BILLY.   Do you mind me coming to sit with you?

ANNIE.   No, not at all.

BILLY.   It doesn't mean we have to talk.

ANNIE.   It's all right.

BILLY.   How do you feel?

ANNIE.   Scared. I'm always scared. I think, this is the one where I get found out.

BILLY.   Well, better in Glasgow.

ANNIE.   Is anyone else on this train?

BILLY.   No, we're completely alone.

ANNIE.   I mean any of *us*, the others.

BILLY.   I don't know. Some of them are flying up, on the shuttle.

ANNIE.   I fancied the train.

BILLY.   I fancied it with you.

ANNIE.   *(Meets his look.)* Billy...

BILLY.   What did you think when you saw me?

ANNIE.   Just now?

BILLY.   No. On the first day.

ANNIE.   I thought God, he's so *young*.

BILLY.   *(Scottish)* I've lived more than you'll ever live.

ANNIE.   All right, all right.

BILLY.   I'm the one who should be scared. You're smashing.

ANNIE.   I don't feel right.

BILLY.   You seem right to me.

ANNIE. I'm older than you.

BILLY. That doesn't matter.

ANNIE. I'm a lot older. I'm going to look more like your mother than your sister.

BILLY. That's all right, so long as it's incest. Anyway, I like older women.

ANNIE. Billy, you mustn't keep flirting with me.

BILLY. Why not?

ANNIE. Well, because there's no point. Will you stop?

BILLY. No. Is that all right?

ANNIE. *(pause)* Did you know I was going to be on this train?

BILLY. *(nods)* Watched you get on. I thought I'd come and find you when it got started.

ANNIE. You certainly thought about it.

BILLY. I had to wait until the inspector came round. I haven't got a first-class ticket.

ANNIE. What will you do if he comes back?

BILLY. I'll say you're my mum. How come you get a first-class ticket?

ANNIE. I don't really. I'm afraid I upped it myself.

BILLY. You approve of the class system?

ANNIE. You mean on trains or in general?

BILLY. In general. Travelling first-class.

ANNIE. There's no system. People group together when they've got something in common. Sometimes it's religion and sometimes it's, I don't know, breeding budgies or being at Eton. Big and small groups overlapping. You can't blame them. It's a cultural thing; it's not *classes* or *system.* *(She makes a connection.)* There's nothing really *there* — it's just the way you see it. Your perception.

BILLY. Bloody brilliant. There's people who've spent their lives trying to get rid of the class system, and you've done it without leaving your seat.

ANNIE. Well...

BILLY. The only problem with your argument is that you've got to be traveling first-class to really appreciate it.

ANNIE. I...

BILLY. Where do you get all that from? Did you just make it up? It's daft. I prefer Brodie. He sounds like rubbish, but you know he's right. You sound all right, but you know it's rubbish.

ANNIE. Why won't you do his play, then?

BILLY. I didn't say I wouldn't. I'll do it if you're doing it.

ANNIE. You shouldn't do it for the wrong reasons.

BILLY. Why not? Does he care?

ANNIE. You said he can't write.

BILLY. He can't write like your husband. But your husband's a first-class writer.

ANNIE. Are you being nasty about Henry?

BILLY. No. I saw *House of Cards*. I thought it was quite good.

ANNIE. He'll be relieved to hear that.

BILLY. *(pause)* Don't go off me.

ANNIE. If you weren't a child, you'd know that you won't get anywhere with a married woman if you're snotty about her husband. Remember that with the next one.

BILLY. I'faith, I mean no harm, sister. I'm just scared sick of you. How is't with ye?

ANNIE. I am very well, brother.

BILLY. Trust me, but I am sick; I fear so sick 'twill cost my life.

ANNIE. Mercy forbid it! 'Tis not so, I hope.

BILLY. I think you love me, sister.

ANNIE. Yes, you know I do.

BILLY. I know't, indeed. You're very fair.

ANNIE. Nay, then, I see you have a merry sickness.

BILLY. That's as it proves. The poets feign, I read,
That Juno for her forehead did exceed
All other goddesses; but I durst swear
Your forehead exceeds hers, as hers did theirs.

ANNIE. 'Troth, this is pretty!

BILLY. Such a pair of stars
As are thine eyes would, like Promethian fire,
If gently glanced, give life to senseless stones.

ANNIE. Fie upon ye!

BILLY. The lily and the rose, most sweetly strange,
Upon your dimpled cheeks do strive for change:
Such lips would tempt a saint; such hands as those
Would make an anchorite lascivious.

ANNIE. O, you are a trim youth!

BILLY. Here! *(His 'reading' has been getting less and less discreet. Now he stands and opens his shirt.)*

ANNIE. *(giggling)* Oh, leave off. *(She looks around nervously.)*

BILLY. *(starting to shout)*
And here's my breast; strike home!
Rip up my bosom; there thou shalt behold

A heart in which is writ the truth I speak.
   ANNIE. You daft idiot.
   BILLY. Yes, most earnest. You cannot love?
   ANNIE. Stop it.
   BILLY. My tortured soul
Hath felt affliction in the heat of death.
Oh, Annabella, I am quite undone!
   ANNIE. Billy!

Scene Three

The living-room of Act One, Scene Two, without all the records.
CHARLOTTE is searching through a file of newspaper cut-
tings and programmes. A large, loaded ruck-sack is sitting
by the door. DEBBIE is smoking.

HENRY. Since when did you smoke?

DEBBIE. I don't know. Years. At school. Me and Terry
used to light up in the boiler room.

HENRY. *I* and Terry.

DEBBIE. I and Terry. Are you sure?

HENRY. It doesn't sound right but it's correct. I paid
school fees so that you wouldn't be barred by your
natural disabilities from being taught Latin and learning
to speak English.

CHARLOTTE. I thought it was so that she'd be a virgin a
bit longer.

HENRY. It was also so that she'd speak English. *Virgo
syntacta.*

DEBBIE. You were done, Henry. Nobody left the boiler
room virgo with Terry.

HENRY. I wish you'd stop celebrating your emancipa-
tion by flicking it at me like a wet towel. Did the staff know
about this lout, Terry?

DEBBIE. He was on the staff. He taught Latin.

HENRY. Oh well, that's all right then.

CHARLOTTE. Apparently she'd already lost it riding anyway.

HENRY. That doesn't count.

CHARLOTTE. In the tackroom.

HENRY. God's truth. The groom.

CHARLOTTE. That's why he was bow-legged.

HENRY. I told you — I said you've got to warn her about being carried away.

DEBBIE. You don't get carried away in jodhpurs. It needs absolute determination.

HENRY. Will you stop this.

CHARLOTTE. No. I can't find it. It was yonks ago. I mean, not being catty, I was nearer the right age.

HENRY. Does it really matter who played Giovanni to your Annabella in 'Tis Pity She's a Whore?

CHARLOTTE. I just think it's awful to have forgotten his name.

DEBBIE. Perhaps he's forgotten yours.

CHARLOTTE. But it was *my* virginity, not his.

DEBBIE. Was it actually on stage?

CHARLOTTE. Don't be silly — it was a British Council tour. No, it was in a boarding house in Zagreb.

DEBBIE. A bawdy house?

CHARLOTTE. The British Council has a lot to answer for.

HENRY. Look, we're supposed to be discussing a family crisis.

CHARLOTTE. What's that?

HENRY. Our daughter going on the streets.

DEBBIE. On the *road*, not the streets.

CHARLOTTE. Stop being so dramatic.

HENRY. I have a right to be dramatic.

CHARLOTTE. I see what you mean.

HENRY. I'm her father.

CHARLOTTE. Oh, I see what you mean.

HENRY. She's too young to go off with a man.

CHARLOTTE. She's certainly too young to go off without one. It's all right. He's nice. *(She has given up her search of the file and now leaves carrying the file. To DEBBIE.)* If I'm in the bath when he comes I want to see you both before you disappear. *(She goes out.)*

HENRY. What does he play? *(DEBBIE looks blank.)* Ma said he's a musician.

DEBBIE. Oh — um — steam organ...

HENRY. A travelling steam organist? *(pause)* He's not a musician.

DEBBIE. Fairground.

HENRY. Well, swings and roundabouts.

DEBBIE. Tunnel of love. How's Annie?

HENRY. In Glasgow.

DEBBIE. Don't worry, Henry, I'll be happy.

HENRY. Happy? What do you mean happy?

DEBBIE. Happy! Like a warm puppy.

HENRY. Dear Christ, is that what it's all come down to? — no philosophy that can't be printed on a T-shirt. You don't get visited by happiness like being lucky with the weather. The weather is the weather.

DEBBIE. And happiness?

HENRY. Happiness is ... equilibrium. Shift your weight.

DEBBIE. Are you happy, Henry?

HENRY. I don't much like your calling me Henry. I liked being called Fa. Fa and Ma.

DEBBIE. Happy days, eh? How're the Everlys getting on? And the Searchers. How's old Elvis?

HENRY. He's dead.

DEBBIE. I did know that. I mean how's he holding up apart from that?

HENRY. I never went for him much. 'All Shook Up' was the last good one. However, I suppose that's the fate of all us artists.

DEBBIE. Death?

HENRY. People saying they preferred the early stuff.

DEBBIE. Well, maybe you were better then.

HENRY. Didn't you like the last one?

DEBBIE. What, *House of Cards*? Well, it wasn't about anything, except did she have it off or didn't she? What a crisis. Infidelity among the architect class. Again.

HENRY. It was about self-knowledge through pain.

DEBBIE. No, it was about did she have it off or didn't she. As if having it off is infidelity.

HENRY. Most people think it is.

DEBBIE. Most people think *not* having it off is *fidelity*. They think all relationships hinge in the middle. Sex or no sex. What a fantastic range of possibilities. Like an on/ off switch. Did she or didn't she? By Henry Ibsen. Why would you want to make it such a crisis?

HENRY. I don't know, why would I?

DEBBIE. It's what comes of making such a mystery of it. I was like that when I was twelve. Everything was sex. Latin was sex. The dictionary fell open at *meretrix*, a harlot. You could feel the mystery coming off the word like musk. *Meretrix!* This was none of your *amo, amas, amat*, this was a flash from the forbidden planet, and it was everywhere. History was sex, French was sex, art was sex, the Bible, poetry, penfriends, games, music, everything was sex except biology which was obviously sex but not *really* sex, not the one which was secret and ecstatic and wicked and a sacrament and all the things it was supposed to be but couldn't be at one and the same time — I got that in the boiler room and it turned out to be biology after all. That's what free love is free of — propaganda.

HENRY. Don't get too good at that.

DEBBIE. What?

HENRY. Persuasive nonsense. Sophistry in a phrase so neat you can't see the loose end that would unravel it. It's flawless but wrong. A perfect dud. You can do that with words, bless 'em. How about 'What free love is free of, is love'? Another little gem. You could put a 'what' on the end of it, like Bertie Wooster, 'What free love is free of is love, what?' — and the words would go on replicating themselves like a spiral of DNA... 'What love is free of love? — *free* love is what love, what?—'

DEBBIE. *(interrupting)* Fa. You're going on.

HENRY. Yes. Well, I remember, the first time I succumbed to the sensation that the universe was dispensable minus one lady—

DEBBIE. Don't write it, Fa. Just say it. The first time you fell in love. What?

HENRY. It's to do with knowing and being known. I remember how it stopped seeming odd that in biblical Greek knowing was used for making love. Whosit knew so-and-so. Carnal knowledge. It's what lovers trust each other with. Knowledge of each other, not of the flesh but through the flesh, knowledge of self, the real him, the real her, *in extremis*, the mask slipped from the face. Every other version of oneself is on offer to the public. We share our vivacity, grief, sulks, anger, joy ... we hand it out to anybody who happens to be standing around, to friends and family with a momentary sense of indecency perhaps, to strangers without hesitation. Our lovers share us with the passing trade. But in pairs we insist that we give ourselves to each other. What selves? What's left? What else is there that hasn't been dealt out like a pack of cards? Carnal knowledge. Personal, final, uncompromised. Knowing, being known. I revere that. Having that is being rich, you can be generous about what's shared — she walks, she talks, she laughs, she lends a sympathetic ear, she kicks off her shoes and dances on the tables, she's everybody's and it don't mean a thing, let them eat cake; knowledge is something else, the undealt card, and while it's held it makes you free-and-easy and nice to know, and when it's gone everything is pain. Every single thing. Every object that meets the eye, a pencil, a tangerine, a travel poster. As if the physical world has been wired up to pass a current back to the part of the brain where imagination glows like a filament in a lobe no bigger than a torch bulb. Pain.

DEBBIE. *(pause)* Has Annie got someone else then?
HENRY. Not as far as I know, thank you for asking.
DEBBIE. Apologies.
HENRY. Don't worry.
DEBBIE. Don't you. Exclusive rights isn't love, it's

colonization.

HENRY. Christ almighty. Another *ersatz* masterpiece. Like Michelangelo working in polystyrene.

DEBBIE. Do you know what your problem is, Henry?

HENRY. What?

DEBBIE. Your Latin mistress never took you into the boiler room.

HENRY. Well, at least I passed.

DEBBIE. Only in Latin.

(Doorbell.)

DEBBIE. Do me a favour.

HENRY. What?

DEBBIE. Stay here.

HENRY. That bad, is he?

DEBBIE. He's frightened of you.

HENRY. Jesus.

(CHARLOTTE enters in a bathrobe, a towel round her hair perhaps. She carries a bunch of postcards.)

CHARLOTTE. Ten postcards — stamped and addressed. Every week I get a postcard you get ten quid. No postcards, no remittance. *(She gives DEBBIE the postcards.)*

DEBBIE. Oh — Charley— *(Kisses CHARLOTTE.)* See you, Henry.

HENRY. There; my blessing with thee. And these few precepts in thy memory...

DEBBIE. Too late, Fa. Love you. *(Kisses him. She leaves with the Ruck-sack followed by CHARLOTTE. HENRY waits until CHARLOTTE returns.)*

CHARLOTTE. What a good job we sold the pony.

HENRY. Musician is he? She's hardly seventeen.

CHARLOTTE. I was in Zagreb when I was seventeen. *(pause)* How's Annie? Are you going to Glasgow for the first night?

HENRY. They don't open for a couple of weeks.

CHARLOTTE. Who's playing Giovanni?

HENRY. I don't know.

CHARLOTTE. Aren't you interested?

HENRY. Should I be?

CHARLOTTE. There's something touching about you, Henry. Everybody should be like you. Not interested. It used to bother me that you were never bothered. Even when I got talked into that dreadful nudie film because it was in Italian and Italian films were supposed to be art... God, that dates me, doesn't it? Debbie's into Australian films. *Australian.* Not Chips Rafferty — actual *films.*

HENRY. You've gone off again.

CHARLOTTE. Yes, well, it didn't bother you so I decided it meant you were having it off right left and centre and it wasn't supposed to matter. By the time I realized you were the last romantic it was too late. I found it *didn't* matter.

HENRY. Well, now that it doesn't... How many — um — roughly how many—?

CHARLOTTE. Nine.

HENRY. *(pause)* Gosh.

CHARLOTTE. And look what your one did compared to my nine.

HENRY. Nine?

CHARLOTTE. Feel betrayed?

HENRY. Surprised. I thought we'd made a commitment.

CHARLOTTE. There are no commitments, only bargains. And they have to be made again every day. You think making a commitment is *it*. Finish. You think it sets like a concrete platform and it'll take any strain you want to put on it. You're committed. You don't have to prove anything. In fact you can afford a little neglect, indulge in a little bit of sarcasm here and there, isolate yourself when you want to. Underneath it's concrete for life. I'm a cow in some ways, but you're an idiot. *Were* an idiot.

HENRY. Better luck next time.

CHARLOTTE. You too. Have a drink?

HENRY. I don't think so, thank you. How are things with your friend? An architect, isn't he?

CHARLOTTE. I had to give him the elbow. Well, he sort of left. I called him the architect of my misfortune.

HENRY. What was the matter with him?

CHARLOTTE. Very possessive type. I came home from a job, I'd been away only a couple of days, and he said, why did I take my diaphragm? He'd been through my bathroom cabinet, would you believe? And then, not finding it, he went through everything else. Can't have that.

HENRY. What did you say?

CHARLOTTE. I said, I didn't *take* my diaphragm, it just went with me. So he said, what about the tube of Duragel? I must admit he had me there.

HENRY. You should have said, 'Duragel! — no wonder the bristles fell out of my toothbrush.'

CHARLOTTE. *(laughs)* Cheers.

HENRY. *(toasting with an empty hand)* Cheers. *(He stands up.)*

CHARLOTTE. Do you have to go?

HENRY. Yes, I ought to.

CHARLOTTE. You don't fancy one for the road?

HENRY. No, really.

CHARLOTTE. Or a drink?

HENRY. *(smiles)* No offence.

CHARLOTTE. Remember what I said.

HENRY. What was that? *(pause)* Oh ... yes. No commitments. Only bargains. The trouble is I don't really believe it. I'd rather be an idiot. It's a kind of idiocy I like. 'I use you because you love me. I love you so use me. Be indulgent, negligent, preoccupied, premenstrual ... your credit is infinite, I'm yours, I'm committed...' It's no trick loving somebody at their *best.* Love is loving them at their worst. Is that romantic? Well, good. Everything should be romantic. Love, work, music, literature, virginity, loss of virginity...

CHARLOTTE. You've still got one to lose, Henry.

(Quiet music begins, continuing without break to the end of Scene Four.)

Scene Four*

An empty space. ANNIE and BILLY are kissing, embracing: wearing rehearsal clothes.

BILLY. Come, Annabella, — no more sister now,
But love, a name more gracious, — do not blush,
Beauty's sweet wonder, but be proud to know
That yielding thou hast conquered, and inflamed
A heart whose tribute is thy brother's life.
ANNIE. And mine is his. O, how these stol'n contents
Would print a modest crimson on my cheeks,
Had any but my heart's delight prevailed!
BILLY. I marvel why the chaster of your sex
Should think this pretty toy called maidenhead
So strange a loss, when, being lost, 'tis nothing,
And you are still the same.
ANNIE. 'Tis well for you;
Now you can talk.
BILLY. Music as well consists
In the ear as in the playing.
ANNIE. O, you're wanton!
Tell on't you're best; do.
BILLY. Thou wilt chide me, then.
Kiss me:— *(He kisses her lightly. She returns the kiss in earnest.)*

*In order to accommodate a scene change, Scene 4 was spoken twice, once as a 'word rehearsal' and then again as an 'acting rehearsal'.

Scene Five

The living-room. HENRY is alone, sitting in a chair, doing no-
thing. It's like the beginning of Scene One and Scene Three of
Act One. ANNIE is heard letting herself in through the front
door. Then she comes in from the hall. ANNIE enters wear-
ing a topcoat and carrying a suitcase and a small
travelling bag.

ANNIE. Hello, I'm back. *(She puts down the suitcase and*
the bag and goes to kiss HENRY.)

HENRY. Hello. *(She starts taking off her coat.)* How was
it?

ANNIE. We had a good finish — a woman in the
audience was sick. Billy came on with my heart skewered
on his dagger and — ugh — whoops! *(She takes her coat out*
into the hall, reappears and goes to the travelling bag.)

HENRY. I thought you were coming back overnight.
(From the travelling bag ANNIE takes a small, smart-looking car-
rier bag with handles, a purchase from a boutique.)

ANNIE. What have you been doing? How's the film?
(She gives the present to HENRY, kissing him lightly.)

HENRY. I thought you were on the sleeper.

ANNIE. What's the matter?

HENRY. I was wondering what happened to you.

ANNIE. Nothing happened to me. Have you had
lunch?

82

HENRY. No. Did you catch the early train this morning, then?

ANNIE. Yes. Scratch lunch, all right? *(She goes onto the kitchen and returns after a moment.)* My God, it's all gone downhill since Sunday. Hasn't Mrs. Chamberlain been?

HENRY. I phoned the hotel.

ANNIE. When?

HENRY. Last night. They said you'd checked out.

ANNIE. Did they? *(She picks up her suitcase and goes out into the bedroom. HENRY doesn't move. A few moments later ANNIE reappears, without the suitcase and almost walking backwards.)* Oh, God, Hen. Have we had burglars? What were you doing?

HENRY. Where were you?

ANNIE. On the sleeper. I don't know why I said I came down this morning. It just seemed easier. I wasn't there last night because I caught the train straight from the theatre.

HENRY. Was the train late arriving?

ANNIE. Do you want to see my ticket?

HENRY. Well, have you been to the zoo? *(She meets his look expressionlessly.)* Who were you with?

ANNIE. Don't be like this, Hen. You're not like this.

HENRY. Yes, I am.

ANNIE. I don't want you to. It's humiliating.

HENRY. I really am not trying to humiliate you.

ANNIE. For you, I mean. It's humiliating for you. *(pause)* I travelled down with one of the company. We had breakfast at Euston Station. He was waiting for a train. I stayed talking. Then I came home, not thinking that suddenly after two and a half years, I'd be asked to account for my movements.

HENRY. You got off the sleeper and spent the morning sitting at Euston Station?

ANNIE. Yes.

HENRY. You and this actor.

ANNIE. Yes. Can I go now? *(She turns away.)*

HENRY. How did you sleep? *(She turns to look at him blankly.)* Well, did you?

ANNIE. Did I what? What's the point? You'd only wonder if I was lying.

HENRY. Would you lie?

ANNIE. I might.

HENRY. Did you?

ANNIE. No. You see? I'm going to tidy up and put everything back.

HENRY. Do you want to know what I was looking for?

ANNIE. No. Did you find it?

HENRY. No. *(She turns towards the bedroom.)*

HENRY. Was it Billy? *(She turns back.)*

ANNIE. Why Billy?

HENRY. I know it's him. Billy, Billy, Billy, the name keeps dropping, each time without significance, but it can't help itself. Hapless as a secret in a computer. Blip, blip. Billy, Billy. Talk to me. I'm sorry about the bedroom.

ANNIE. You should have put everything back. Everything would be the way it was.

HENRY. You can't put things back. They won't go back. Talk to me. I'm your chap. I know about this. We start off like one of those caterpillars designed for a particular leaf. The exclusive voracity of love. And then not. Hòw strange that the way of things is not suspended to meet our special case. But it never is. I don't want anyone else but sometimes, surprisingly, there's someone, not the prettiest or the most available, but you know that in another life it would be her. Or him, don't you find? A small quickening. The room responds slightly to being entered. Like a raised blind. Nothing intended, and a long way from doing anything, but you catch the glint of being someone else's possibility, and it's a sort of politeness to show you haven't missed it, so you push it a little, well within safety, but there's that sense of a promise almost being made in the touching and kissing without which no one can seem to say good morning in this poncy business and one more push would do it. Billy. Right?

ANNIE. Yes.

HENRY. I love you.

ANNIE. And I you. I wouldn't be here if I didn't.

HENRY. Tell me, then.

ANNIE. I love you.

HENRY. Not that.

ANNIE. Yes, that. That's all I'd need to know.

HENRY. You'd need more.

ANNIE. No.

HENRY. I need it. I can manage knowing if you did but I can't manage not knowing if you did or not. I won't be able to work.

ANNIE. Don't blackmail.

HENRY. You'd ask me.

ANNIE. I never have.

HENRY. There's never *been* anything.

ANNIE. Dozens.

HENRY. In your head.

ANNIE. What's the difference? For the first year at least, every halfway decent looking woman under fifty you were ever going to meet.

HENRY. But you learned better.

ANNIE. No, I just learned not to care. There was nothing to keep you here so I assumed you wanted to stay. I stopped caring about the rest of it.

HENRY. I care. Tell me.

ANNIE. *(hardening)* I did tell you. I spent the morning talking to Billy in a station cafeteria instead of coming straight home to you and I fibbed about the train because *that* seemed like infidelity — but all you want to know is did I sleep with him first?

HENRY. Yes. Did you?

ANNIE. No.

HENRY. Did you want to?

ANNIE. Oh, for God's sake!

HENRY. You can ask me.

ANNIE. I prefer to respect your privacy.

HENRY. I have none. I disclaim it. Did you?

ANNIE. What about your dignity, then?

HENRY. Yes, you'd behave better than me. I don't believe in behaving well. I don't believe in debonair relationships. 'How's your lover today, Amanda?' 'In the pink, Charles. How's yours?' I believe in mess, tears, pain, self-abasement, loss of self-respect, nakedness. Not caring doesn't seem much different from not loving. Did you? You did, didn't you?

ANNIE. This isn't caring. If I had an affair, it would be out of need. Care about that. You can't play on my guilt or my remorse. I'd have none.

HENRY. Need? What did you talk about?

ANNIE. Brodie mostly.

HENRY. Yes. I had it coming.

ANNIE. Billy wants to do Brodie's play.

HENRY. When are you going to see Billy again?

ANNIE. He's going straight into another show. I promised to see him. I want to see him.

HENRY. Fine, when should we go? It's all right to come with you, is it?

ANNIE. Why not? Don't let me out of your sight, eh, Hen?

HENRY. When were you thinking of going?

ANNIE. I thought the weekend.

HENRY. And where is it?

ANNIE. Well, Glasgow.

HENRY. Billy travelled down with you from Glasgow and then took a train back?

ANNIE. Yes.

HENRY. And I'm supposed to score points for dignity. I don't think I can. It'll become my only thought. It'll replace thinking.

ANNIE. You mustn't do that. You have to find a part of yourself where I'm not important or you won't be worth loving. It's awful what you did to my clothes and everything. I mean what you did to yourself. It's not you. And it's you I love.

HENRY. Actually I don't think I can manage the

weekend. I hope it goes well.

ANNIE. Thank you. *(She moves towards the bedroom.)*

HENRY. What does Billy think of Brodie's play?

ANNIE. He says he can't write. *(She leaves. HENRY takes his present out of its bag. It is a tartan scarf.)*

Scene Six

ANNIE sits reading on the train. BILLY approaches the seat next to ANNIE. He speaks with a Scottish accent. He carries a grip. The dialogue is amplified through a mike.

BILLY. Excuse me, is this seat taken?

ANNIE. No.

BILLY. Mind if I sit down?

ANNIE. It's a free country.

BILLY. *(Sits down.)* D'you reckon?

ANNIE. Sorry?

BILLY. You reckon it's a free country? *(ANNIE ignores him.)* Going far?

ANNIE. To London.

BILLY. All the way. *(ANNIE starts to move to an empty seat.)* I'll let you read.

ANNIE. Thank you. *(She sits in the empty seat.)*

BILLY. My name's Bill. *(She ignores him.)* Can I just ask you one question?

ANNIE. Mary.

BILLY. Can I just ask you one question, Mary?

ANNIE. One.

BILLY. Do you know what time this train is due to arrive in London?

ANNIE. At about half-past one, I believe, if it's on time.

89

BILLY. You put me in mind of Mussolini, Mary. People used to say Mussolini, he may be a Fascist, but—

ANNIE. No — that's wrong — that's the old script—

BILLY. *(Swears under his breath.)* Sorry, Roger...

ROGER. *(voice off)* Okay, cut the tape.

ANNIE. From the top, Roger?

ROGER. *(voice off)* Give us a minute.

(A light change reveals that the setting is a fake, in a TV studio. ANNIE gets up and moves away. BILLY joins her. They exchange a few words, and she moves back to her seat, leaving him estranged, an unhappy feeling between them. After a moment the scene fades out.)

Scene Seven

HENRY is alone listening to the radio, which is playing Bach's Air
on a G string. ANNIE enters from the bedroom, dressed to
go out, and she is in a hurry.

HENRY. *(urgently, on seeing her)* Listen—
ANNIE. I can't. I'm going to be late now.
HENRY. It's important. *Listen.*
ANNIE. What?
HENRY. *Listen. (She realizes that he means the radio. She lis-*
tens for a few moments.) What is it?
ANNIE. *(pleased)* Do you like it?
HENRY. I *love* it.
ANNIE. *(congratulating him)* It's Bach.
HENRY. The cheeky beggar.
ANNIE. What?
HENRY. He's stolen it.
ANNIE. *Bach?*
HENRY. Note for note. Practically a straight lift from
Procul Harum. And he can't even get it right. Hang on.
I'll play the original. *(He moves to get the record.)*
ANNIE. *(Pleased by him but going, moves to him.)* Work well.
(She kisses him quickly and lightly.)
HENRY. *(He forces the kiss into a less casual one. His voice,*
however, keeps its detachment.) You too.

ANNIE. Last day. Why don't you come? *(HENRY shrugs.)* No, all right.

HENRY. I'm only the ghost writer anyway.

(The phone rings.)

ANNIE. If that's them, say I've left.

HENRY. *(into the phone)* She's left... Oh... *(to ANNIE)* It's your friend. *(She hesitates.)* Just go.

ANNIE. *(Takes the phone. Into phone.)* Billy...? Yes — what? — yes, of course— I'm just late — yes — goodbye — all right... Yes, fine. Good-bye. *(She hangs up.)* I love you. Do you understand?

HENRY. No.

ANNIE. Do you think it's unfair?

HENRY. No. It's as though I've been careless, left a door open somewhere while preoccupied.

ANNIE. I'll stop.

HENRY. Not for me. I won't be the person who stopped you. I can't be that. When I got upset you said you'd stop so I try not to get upset. I don't get pathetic because when I got pathetic I could feel how tedious it was, how unattractive. Like Max, your ex. Remember Max? Love me because I'm in pain. No good. Not in very good taste. So. Dignified cuckoldry is a difficult trick, but it can be done. Think of it as modern marriage. We have got beyond hypocrisy, you and I. Exclusive rights isn't love, it's colonization.

ANNIE. Stop it — please stop it.

HENRY. *(pause)* The trouble is, I can't *find* a part of myself where you're not important. I write in order to be

worth your while and to finance the way I want to live
with you. Not the way *you* want to live. The way *I* want to
live with *you.* Without you I wouldn't care. I'd eat tinned
spaghetti and put on yesterday's clothes. But as it is I
change my socks, and make money, and tart up Brodie's
unspeakable drivel into speakable drivel so he can be an
author too, like me. Not that it will do him much good. A
touch meretricious. *Meretrix, meretricis.* Harlot.

ANNIE. You shouldn't have done it if you didn't think
it was right.

HENRY. You think it's right. I can't cope with more
than one moral system at a time. Mine is that what you
think is right is right. What you do is right. What you want
is right. There was a tribe, wasn't there, which wor-
shipped Charlie Chaplin. It worked just as well as any
other theology, apparently. They loved Charlie Chaplin.
I love you.

ANNIE. So you'll forgive me anything, is that it, Hen?
I'm a selfish cow but you love me so you'll overlook it, is
that right? Thank you, but that's not it. I wish I felt selfish,
everything would be easy. Goodbye Billy. I don't need
him. How can I need someone I spend half my time telling to grow up? I'm... — what's a petard?, I've often
wondered.

HENRY. What?

ANNIE. A petard. Something you hoist, is it, piece
of rope?

HENRY. I don't think so.

ANNIE. Well, anyway. All right?

HENRY. All right what? I keep marrying people who

suddenly lose a wheel.

ANNIE. I don't feel selfish, I feel hoist. I send out waves, you know. Not free. Not interested. He sort of got in under the radar. Acting daft on a train. Next thing I'm looking round for him, makes the day feel better, it's like love or something: no — love, absolutely, how can I say it wasn't? You weren't replaced, or even replaceable. But I liked it, being older for once, in charge, my pupil. And it was a long way north. And so on. I'm sorry I hurt you. But I meant it. It meant something. And now that it means less than I thought and I feel silly, I won't drop him as if it was nothing, a pick-up, it wasn't that, I'm not that. I just want him to stop needing me so I can stop behaving well. This is me behaving well. I have to choose who I hurt and I choose you because I'm yours. *(pause)*

(The phone rings.)

ANNIE. Maybe it's just me.

HENRY. *(into phone)* Roger—? She's left, about ten minutes ago — yes, I know, dear, but — don't talk to me about unprofessional, Roger — you lost half a day shooting the war memorial with a boom shadow all over it — okay, scream at me if it makes you feel better—

ANNIE. *(Takes the phone out of his hand. Into phone.)* Keep your knickers on, it's only a bloody play. *(She hangs up and starts to go. Going.)* Bye.

HENRY. Annie. *(pause)* Yes, all right.

ANNIE. I need you.

HENRY. Yes, I know.

ANNIE. Please, don't let it wear away what you feel for me. It won't, will it?

HENRY. No, not like that. It will go on or it will flip into its opposite. What time will you be back?

ANNIE. Not late. *(He nods at her. She nods back and leaves.)*

HENRY. *(He sits down in his chair. Then he gets up and starts the record playing — Procul Harum's 'A Whiter Shade of Pale', which is indeed a version of 'Air on a G String'. He stands listening to it, smiling at its Bach, until the vocals start. Then the smile gets overtaken.)* Oh, please, please, please, please, *don't.*

(Then blackout, but the music continues.)

Scene Eight

*In the blackout the music gives way to recorded dialogue between
ANNIE and BILLY, who speaks with a Scottish accent.*

BILLY. *(voice)* Wait for me.

ANNIE. *(voice)* Yes, I will.

BILLY. *(voice)* Everything's got to change. Except you.
Don't you change.

ANNIE. *(voice)* No, I won't. I'll wait for you and for
everything to change.

BILLY. *(voice)* That could take longer. *(laughs)* I might
have to do it myself.

*(By this time, light has appeared starting with the faint glow from
the television screen. BRODIE, alone in the living-room, is
twenty-five, wearing a cheap suit. He is holding a tumbler of
neat scotch, his attention engaged by the television set and
particularly by the accompanying video machine. From the
television the dialogue has been followed by the echoing clang
of a cell door, footsteps, credit music ... BRODIE turns the
volume down. HENRY enters from the kitchen carrying a
small jug of water for BRODIE's scotch. In the room there is
wine for HENRY and another glass for ANNIE. HENRY
switches off the TV and removes the video cassette.)*

BRODIE. *(with a Scottish accent)* Very handy, these

machines. When did they come out?

HENRY. Well, I suppose they were coming out about the time you were going in.

BRODIE. You can set them two weeks ahead.

HENRY. Yes.

BRODIE. How much?

HENRY. A few hundred. They vary.

BRODIE. I'll have to pinch one sometime.

HENRY. If you leave it a bit, they'll probably improve them so that you can have it recording concurrently with your sentence.

BRODIE. *(Looks at HENRY without expression.)* Annie looked nice. She's come on a bit since *Rosie of the Royal Infirmary.* A good-looking woman. *(HENRY doesn't answer.)*

(ANNIE enters from the kitchen with a dip, peanuts, etc. on a tray. She puts the tray down. HENRY pours wine into a third glass.)

BRODIE. Just saying, you look nice.

ANNIE. Oh, yes?

BRODIE. The pretty one was supposed to be me, was he?

ANNIE. Well...

BRODIE. He's not a pansy, is he?

ANNIE. I don't think so. *(HENRY hands her the glass of wine.)* Thank you.

HENRY. *(to BRODIE, indicating the TV)* What did you think?

BRODIE. I liked it better before. You don't mind me saying?

HENRY. No.

ANNIE. It did work.

BRODIE. You mean getting me sprung?

ANNIE. No, I didn't mean that.

BRODIE. That's right. I got sprung by the militarists.

HENRY. I don't think I follow that.

BRODIE. Half a billion pounds for defence, nothing left for prisons. So you get three, four to a cell. First off, they tell the magistrates, for God's sake go easy, *fine* the bastards. But still they keep coming — four, five to a cell. Now they're frightened it's going to blow up. Even the warders are going on strike. So: 'Give us the money to build more prisons!' 'Can't be done, laddie, we're spending the money to keep the world free, not in prison.' So they start freeing the prisoners. Get it? I'm out because the missiles I was marching against are using up the money they need for a prison to put me in. Beautiful. Can I have another? *(He holds up his empty glass for ANNIE. Slight pause. HENRY stays still.)*

ANNIE. Please help yourself.

BRODIE. *(He does so.)* Early release. There was eight of us just on my corridor. *(to HENRY)* Not one of them a controversial TV author. I don't owe you.

HENRY. Is it against your principles to say thank you for *anything*, even a drink?

BRODIE. Fair enough. You had a go. You did your best. It probably needed something, to work in with their prejudices.

HENRY. Yes, they are a bit prejudiced, these drama producers. They don't like plays which go 'clunk' every time someone opens his mouth. They gang up against soap-box bigots with no idea that everything has a length. They think TV is a visual medium. *(to ANNIE, puzzled)* Is this *him?*

BRODIE. Don't be clever with me, Henry, like you were clever with my play. I lived it and put my guts into it, and you came along and wrote it clever. Not for me. For her. I'm not stupid.

ANNIE. *(to HENRY)* No, this isn't him.

BRODIE. Yes, it bloody is. That was me on the train, and this is me again, and I don't think you're that different either.

ANNIE. And *that* wasn't him. *(She points at the TV.)* He was helpless, like a three-legged calf, nervous as anything. A boy on the train. Chatting me up. Nice. He'd been in some trouble at the camp, some row, I forget, he was going absent without leave. He didn't know anything about a march. He didn't know anything about anything, except *Rosie of the Royal Infirmary.* By the time we got to London he would have followed me into the Ku Klux Klan. He tagged on. And when we were passing the war memorial he got his lighter out. It was one of those big chrome Zippos — click, snap. Private Brodie goes over the top to the slaughter, not an idea in his head except to impress me. What else could I do? He was my recruit.

HENRY. You should have told me. That one I would have known how to write.

ANNIE. Yes.

BRODIE. Listen — I'm still here.

ANNIE. So you are, Bill. Finish your drink, will you?

BRODIE. Why not? *(He finishes his drink and stands up.)* I can come back for some dip another time. *(He picks up the bowl of dip and hands it to ANNIE.)*

ANNIE. No time like the present. *(She takes the bowl of dip and smashes it into his face. She goes to the hall door, leaving it open while she briefly disappears to get BRODIE's coat. HENRY has stood up, but BRODIE isn't going to do anything. He carefully wipes his face with his handkerchief.)*

HENRY. Well, it was so interesting to meet you. I'd heard so much about you.

BRODIE. I don't really blame you, Henry. The price was right. I remember the time she came to visit me. She was in a blue dress, and there was a thrill coming off her like she was back on the box, but there was no way in. It was the first time I felt I was in prison. You know what I mean. *(ANNIE stands at the door holding BRODIE's coat. He takes it from her, ignoring her as he walks out. She follows him, and the front door is heard closing. ANNIE returns.)*

HENRY. I don't know what it did to him, but it scared the hell out of me. Are you all right?

ANNIE. *(She nods.)* Are you all right?

(The phone rings.)

HENRY. *(He picks it up.)* Hello. *(into the phone, suddenly uncomfortable)* Oh, hello. Did you want to speak to Annie?

ANNIE. No.

HENRY. *(suddenly relaxes)* Well, that's fantastic, Max! *(to ANNIE)* It's your ex. He's getting married. *(to phone)* Congratulations. Who is she? *(HENRY ferries this over to ANNIE with an expressive look, which she returns. ANNIE moves to HENRY and embraces his shoulders from behind. She leans on him tiredly while he deals with the phone.)* Oh, I think you're very wise. To marry one actress is unfortunate, to marry two is simply asking for it. *(ANNIE kisses him. He covers the mouthpiece with his hand. Into phone.)* Really? Across a crowded room, eh?

ANNIE. I've had it. Look after me.

HENRY. *(He covers the mouthpiece.)* Don't worry. I'm your chap. *(into phone)* Well, it's very decent of you to say so, Max. *(to ANNIE)* 'No hard feelings?' What does he mean? If it wasn't for me, he wouldn't be engaged *now*. *(ANNIE disengages herself from him with a smile and goes around turning out the lights until the only light is coming from the bedroom door. Into phone.)* No. I'm afraid she isn't... She'll be so upset when I tell her... No, I mean when I tell her she missed you... No, she'll be delighted. I'm delighted, Max. Isn't love wonderful? *(ANNIE finishes with the lights and goes out into the bedroom. HENRY is being impatiently patient with MAX on the phone, trying to end it.)* Yes, well, we look forward to meeting her. What? Oh, yes? *(Absently he clicks on the little radio.)*

(The radio starts playing, softly, 'I'm a Believer' by the Monkees.)

HENRY. *(He is immediately beguiled. He forgets MAX until the phone crackle gets back through to him.)* Sorry. Yes, I'm still here. *(He turns the song up slightly.)*

COSTUME PLOT

HENRY

Act One, Scene2:
> Gray cord shirt
> Tan pants
> Webbed belt w/ leather trim
> Brown socks
> Tan lace-up shoes
> Watch
> Wedding ring #1
> Hanky
> Glasses

Act One, Scene 4:
> Burgundy shirt
> Green cord pants
> Grey crewneck sweater
> Argyl socks
> Brown boots
> Green/rust scarf
> Grey poplin coat
> Brown gloves

Act Two, Scene 1:
> Tweed slacks
> Coral w/ blue stripe shirt
> Rust knit tie
> Rusty mauve sweater vest
> Brown socks
> Tan lace-up shoes
> Tweed jacket used as props
> Wedding ring #2

Act Two, Scene 3
> Grey cotton shirt
> Grey cord pants
> Green tweed jacket
> Tan sleeveless jacket
> Taupe knit tie ˙
> Navy cashmere coat
> Brown socks
> Tan lace-up shoes

Act Two, Scene 5:
> Brown plaid robe

Act Two, Scene 7:
> Dark green shirt
> Grey cord pants
> Mauve cable-knit sweater
> Brown socks
> Brown loafers

Act Two, Scene 8:
> Dark green shirt
> Red knit tie
> Rusty mauve sweater vest
> Grey cord pants
> Brown socks
> Brown loafers

ANNIE

Act One, Scene 2:
> Grey skirt, pink sweater rig
> Grey blazer w/ "Free Brodie" button
> Purple scarf
> Grey suede boots

Maroon cashmere cape
Maroon leather bag
Watch #1
Wedding ring #1
Grey short poplin jacket

Act One, Scene 3:
Green cord pants w/ suspenders
Beige t-shirt / tan t-shirt
Mint green socks
Alligator flats
Watch

Act One, Scene 4:
Brown plaid robe
Cream satin tap pants

Act Two, Scene 1:
Eggplant coulottes
Brown / white small-checked man's shirt
Purple socks
Wedding ring #2
Watch #2

Act Two, Scene 3:
White / peach sweater
Camel wool slacks
Grey poplin raincoat
Rust boots w/ velcro
Purple socks
Brown suede bag

Act Two, Scene 4:
Oatmeal rehearsal skirt
Green man's shirt w/ blue sweatshirt rig
Black ballet slippers

Act Two, Scene 6:
     Burberry trench coat
     Maroon challis print scarf
     Grey short boots
     Gloves
     Rust shoulder bag
Act Two, Scene 7:
     Rust skirt / blouse
     Rust coat w/ vest rig
     Rust boots
     Brown leather bag
     Scarf
     Slate grey hose
Act Two, Scene 8:
     Peach chenille sweater
     Rust skirt
     Wine socks
     Rust flats

MAX

Act One, Scene 1:
     Black silk pajamas
     Black paisley silk robe w/ white hanky
     Black velvet slippers
     Cigarette case
     Passport
Act One, Scene 2:
     Green kaiki pants
     Maroon long-sleeve polo shirt
     T-shirt
     Athletic socks

Running shoes
Web belt
Grey poplin jacket
Act One, Scene 3:
Green sweat pants
White t-shirt
Athletic socks
Olive velour robe
Bloody hanky

CHARLOTTE

Act One, Scene 1:
Black / grey dress rig w/ tie
Black wool coat
Black gloves
Black patent shoes
Grey bag
Grey hose
Earrings
Watch
Act One, Scene 2:
Grey sweat pants w/ leg-warmers
Rust socks
Brown plaid robe
change
Grey sweat pants w/ leg-warmers
Light beige sweater
Black ballet slippers
Rust socks
Act Two, Scene 3:
Green suede pants

Mint green cashmere sweater
Dark green shoes
Turquoise necklace & bracelet
   change
Peach silk robe
Towel

DEBBIE

Act Two, Scene 3:
   Grey mini skirt
   Yellow / black t-shirt
   Blue 40's jacket
   Black cinch belt
   Brown cowboy boots
   Green hose over cobalt blue

BILLY

Act Two, Scene 2:
   Blue denim western shirt
   Black jeans
   Black athletic shoes
   Blue socks
   Blue jacket
Act Two, Scene 4:
   White rehearsal shirt
   Black jeans
   Black boots
Act Two, Scene 6:
   Green checked jacket
   Black tapered t-shirt
   Green slacks
   Black lace-up boots

BRODIE

Act Two, Scene 8:

>   Blue 2-piece cheap suit
>   Green print shirt
>   Black t-shirt
>   Black lace-up shoes
>   Grey work socks
>   Black / white top coat

PROPS

Act One, Scene One:
Architect's Drawing board
T square, etc on board
Stool
Pedestal for hotel model
Model
Wedge for booze
Bombay gin
Stoly
Vermouth
Glass
Small suitcase (OSR)
Glass ball with alps in white bag, wrapped in tissue (OSR)
Small table (CS)
Chair (CS)
Trick cards on table (CS)
Passport (Max's pocket)
Silver bowl with pretzels (on table)
Silver ashtray (on table)
Lighter (on table)
Red and black pencils on drawing board

Act One, Scene Two:
Rug
Couch
Two end tables
Two lamps
Pouff (SR of trunk)
Albums (on couch, SL of trunk)

Newspapers (on trunk, SR and SL of trunk)
Four pillows (on couch)
Trunk
3 ashtrays
    Coffee table
    Lower level of both end tables
Record player
Speakers
Records (two shelves of SL bookshelves)
Album on record player
Album cover (SR prop table)
Collected plays in bookshelves
Fireplace fender, newspaper on DS fender
2 coffee mugs (on trunk)
Coffee thermos (on trunk)
Wine glasses and tumbler (SR bookshelf)
Napkins (SR bookshelf)
5th album in (SL bookshelf) "Skaters Waltz"
Paper grocery bag with veges, SL prop table
Crudites (SR prop table)
Bowl with dip (SR prop table)
Hawaiian pineapple tin with dip (SR prop table)
Blood (SR)
Bloodstained hankie (OSR)
Orange juice container, two-thirds full (OSR)
Champagne bottle, filled with ginger ale (OSR)
Clean hankie (Henry — personal prop)
HOUSE OF CARDS poster (SL bookshelf)
PLAYER'S GUIDE, magazine, (OSL) Max carries on
Cigarettes, matches (coffee table,, mantel, lower level of
    end tables)
Window blind (2/3's of the way up)

Act One, Scene Three:
Couch with throw
Round end table with table cloth (US of couch)
Radio (DS of couch)
Chinese coffee table (in front of couch)
Oriental rug (beneath coffee table)
Rag rug (beneath coffee table)
Rag rug (L of CS)
Rocking chair (on rag rug)
Bloodstained, hard hankie (Max's pocket)
White wine bottle (SR of rocking chair, half full,
    corked)
Wine glass, next to bottle
MARS bar, personal prop, Annie
German poster on wall behind couch
Photo of Annie, Candle holder, phone and Chinese box
    on round end table
Ladies head with flowers (in wall piece)
Books to cover electrical outlet (beneath radio)
Tiffany lamp (SR of window) on high round table
Basket of flowers (SL of window)

Act One, Scene Four:
Futon couch
Desk chair (SL)
Fle cabinet desk (SL)
Mantel w/ books, mug, dead rose, candle sticks
Cardboard packing boxes, either side of futon
Newspapers and magazines on boxes

On desk:
>   Paperback books
>   Scripts
>   Writing paper and pencil
>   Mug w/ coffee
>   Toast on plate
>   Clock
>   Lamp
>   Typewriter
>   Cassette player w/cassette inside
>   Paper inside typewriter (2/3 typed on)
>   Miranda Jessop postcard

"Miss Julie" script on top of Annie's carton (SL)
Cassettes (in Annie's carton)
File box w/personal letter (on floor DS of desk)
Flat file box beneath letter box
Other file boxes DS of fireplace
Heater SR and DS of futon (not working)
Telephone (on boxes SL of futon)
Wastepaper basket US of desk
Poster above fireplace
Annie suitcase (same as Act Two, Scene 2) on top of
   boxes
Trunk (SL of futon)
Lampshade SR and DS of boxes
Radiator SR of boxes
Annie photo on windowsill
Half drunk glass of wine on windowsill
Dropcloth and roller and pan in front of radiator
Personal props HENRY:
>   Coat
>   Boots
>   Scarf

Act Two, Scene One:
Curtains closed
Desk DS of window
On desk:
>Telephone
>Photo of Annie
>Photo of Debbie
>Small box
>Typewriter
>Kronk and Zadok script page in typewriter
>Writing paper SL of typewriter
>Cassette player
>Cigarettes and matches
>Ashtray
>Book
>Empty coffee cup

Wastepaper basket, DS and SR of desk
Brodie script on wastepaper basket w/ pencil marker
In desk drawers
>Kronk and Zadok scripts pages
>Penknife
>Pencils

2 bookshelves:
>Albums
>Turntable
>Speakers
>Old books
>Lamps
>Bar w/glasses, scotch bottle, ice bucket

Album on turntable
Desk chair at desk

Brown couch
Paisley throw with "dramatic corner" on couch
Oriental rug beneath couch
Books on floor SR and SL of desk
2 plants on floor SR and SL of desk
Coffee table in front of couch
On coffee table:
> Wicker coffee jug
> Books
> Bowl of fruit, inc. fresh grapes
> Mug
> Ashtray (2)
> Cigarettes and matches
> Paper napkins
> Candlestick
> Lighter

Books beneath coffee table
Henry and Charlotte Cricket Painting in new frame over mantel
Log basket US of fireplace with logs
Fire tools (DS of fireplace)
Log fire
2 stands US of fireplace with plants
Poster of "House of Cards" SL bookshelf above turntable
Easy chair SL and DS
Pouff in front of chair
Cricket bat (OSL in hall)
Cookies on plate OSL
EMMA on chair — open — ANNIE is reading
Empty sleeve for album to go in (with albums)

Act Two, Scene Two:

Billy's travel bag

Annie's luggage over seat

Annie's raincoat and book (GOOD BEHAVIOR) on
   train seat — personal prop

TIS PITY script — in Annie's purse

Memorabilia box on floor CS

> Photos
> Folders
> Dried rose
> Theatre programs
> Ballet slippers

Mug, ashtray, cigarettes, matches c/s next to box

Cigarettes and matches on mantel and coffee table

On coffee table / trunk:

> Mug
> Beer bottle and glass
> 2 granola bars
> Book
> Sunglasses
> Carton of Mores
> Ashtrays
> Runner

Rucksack (SR end of couch)

Scarf behind rucksack

Easy chair CS

Window shade down

Altered bookshelves from Act I, Sc. 2

> Trophies
> Scripts struck
> More photos
> Albums added (Classical)
> Brass vases

Mantel altered
> Other photos
> Brass vases w/feathers
> Ashtray US end
> Brass sugar bowl

New plant US of fender
Book SR end table
Pouff SL corner of pallet
10 addressed postcards OSR
Check for fluff on floor and lampshades straight

Act Two, Scene Four:
Billy's bag

Act Two, Scene Five:
Annie's suitcase OSL
Black giftbox OSL w/ Annie's purse, tartan scarf
inside box
Strike boots on floor SR and SL of desk
Strike wastepaper basket
Open curtains
Add Sunday papers on coffee table and beneath
Change plants on stand
Matches on desk only
Pair of men's pants over arm of couch
Strike log basket
Strike log on fire

Act Two, Scene Six:
Cigarettes and lighter — Annie's coat pocket — personal prop

Book for Annie to read — personal prop

Act Two, Scene seven:
Script pages beneath book on coffee table
Album on turntable — playing
Procal Harum album
Strike papers, scarf, etc.
Change plants
TV set SR of desk

Act Two, Scene Eight:
Two glasses OSL — actors carry on
Bottle wine OSL — Actor carry on
Tray with chips and dip OSL — Actor carry on
Tray with peanuts and pretzels — actor carry on (OSL)
  dip in styrofoam bowl
Scotch in tumbler on bar
Glass OSR w/Scotch in it — Brodie carry on
TV set and VCR set on (propman)
Close curtains (propman during blackout)
Brodie coat OSL in hall — personal prop

GENERAL NOTES:
Thousands of London papers
Napkins and/or kleenex on sets for frequent spills
Lots of backup glasses and mugs
Backup champagne bottles (perhaps varnished labels —
  to prevent peeling from bottle sweating)
British cigarettes packages
Specific albums
Specific books

TIS PITY and MISS JULIE scripts — lots of them
Lots of Brodie script covers
Sleeves for albums
For fake fire — replacement charred logs
Lots of brown grocery bags and white carry-on bags
Tissue paper
Extra Paisley for dip spills
Recipes for dips
Ginger Ale
OJ
Veges
Beer

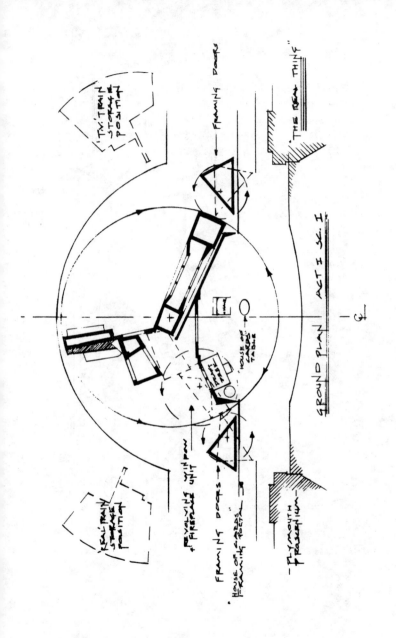

GROUND PLAN   ACT II Sc. I

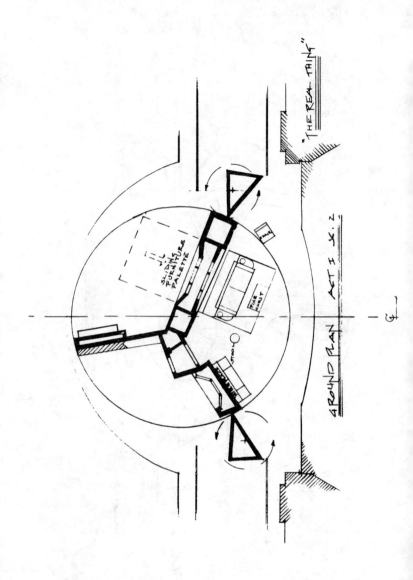

"THE REAL THING"

GROUND PLAN   ACT II sc. 2

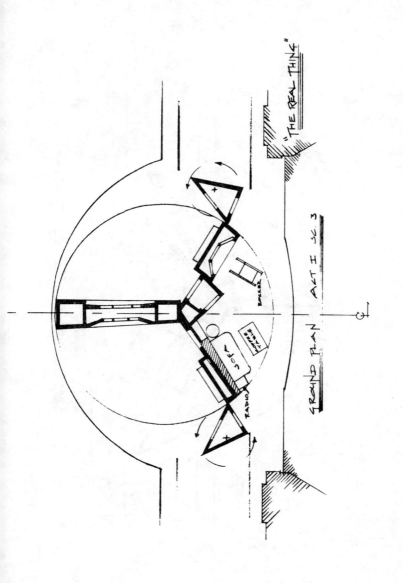

"THE REAL THING"

GROUND PLAN   ACT II SC. 3

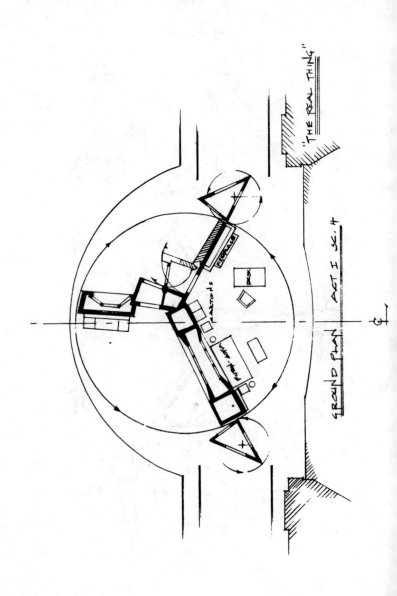

GROUND PLAN   ACT I   Sc. 4

"THE REAL THING"

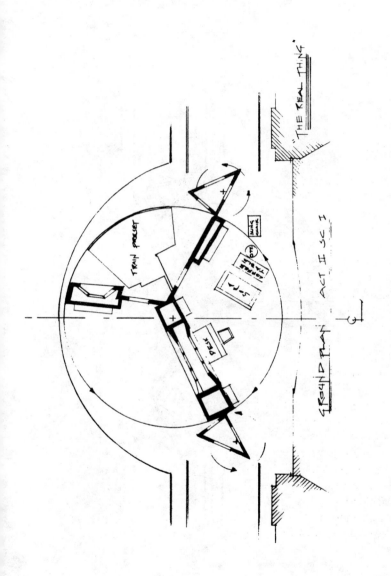

GROUND PLAN   ACT II SC 1

"THE REAL THING"

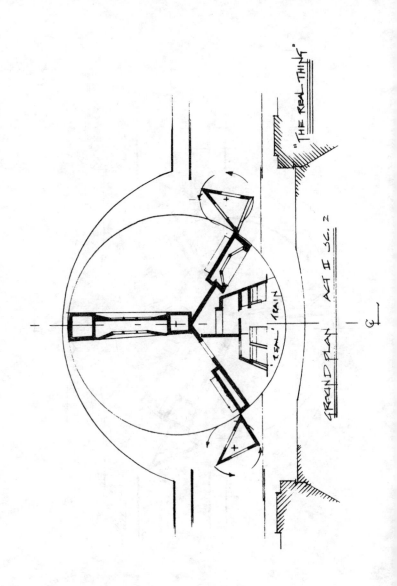

'REAL' TRAIN

GROUND PLAN   ACT II SC. 2

"THE REAL THING"

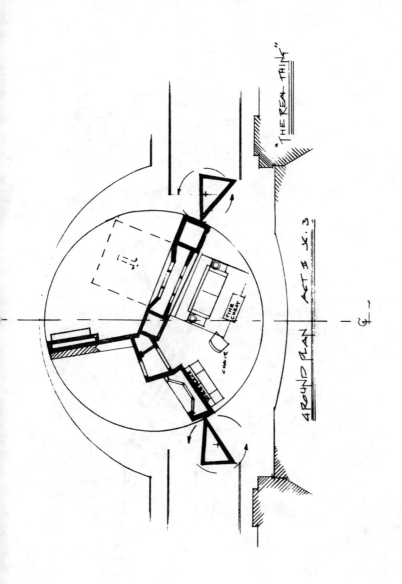

GROUND PLAN   ACT II x. 3

"THE REAL THING"

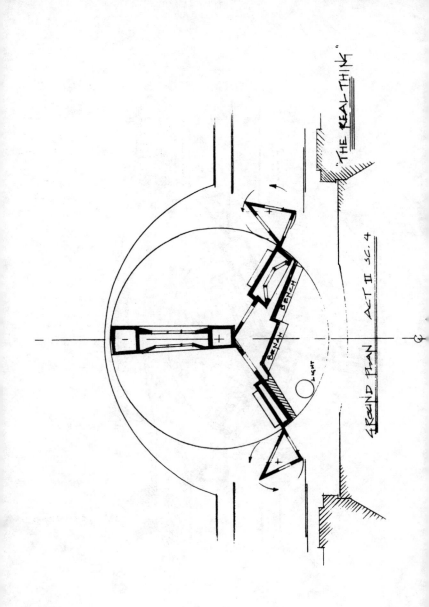

GROUND PLAN   ACT II SC. 4   "THE REAL THING"

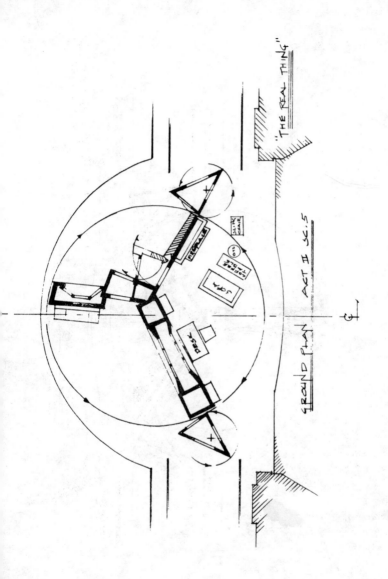

GROUND PLAN   ACT II SC.5

"THE REAL THING"

SOFA

GENERAL TABLE

DESK

DESK CHAIR

FIREPLACE

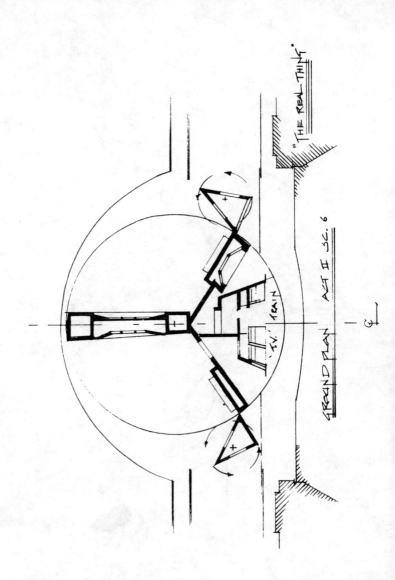

GROUND PLAN · ACT II SC. 6

"THE REAL THING"

T.V. TRAIN

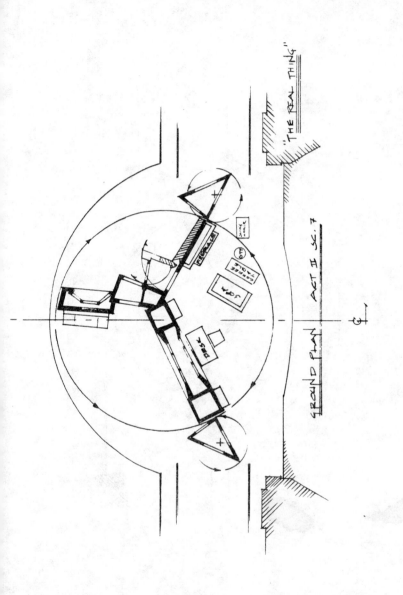

GROUND PLAN — ACT II SC. 7

"THE REAL THING"

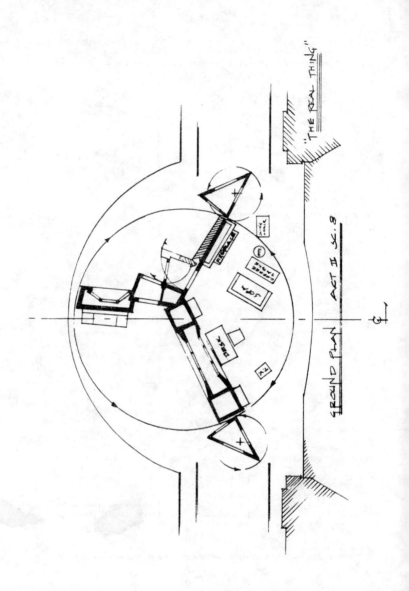

GROUND PLAN — ACT II sc. 9

"THE REAL THING"

Other Publications for Your Interest

KNOCK KNOCK
(LITTLE THEATRE—FARCE)

By JULES FEIFFER

3 men, 1 woman—Composite interior

Take a pair of old Jewish bachelor recluses, throw in Joan of Arc who also in another life was Cinderella—add another character who appears in various guises and you have the entire cast but not the story of this wild farce. Cohn, an atheistic ex-musician is the house-keeper "half" of this "odd couple." Abe, an agnostic ex-stockbroker is the practical "half." They have lived together for twenty years—are bored to tears with one another and constantly squabble. Cohn, exasperated, wishes for intelligent company and on the scene enters one Wiseman who appears in many roles and is part Mephistopheles, part Groucho Marx. Then Joan of Arc appears before the couple telling them her mission is to recruit two of every species for a spaceship trip to heaven. After that all antic hell breaks loose and continues to the mad ending. ". . . a wild spree of jokes . . . helium-light laughter."—Clive Barnes, N.Y. Times. ". . . a kooky, laugh-saturated miracle play in the absurdist tradition."—Time. ". . . grand fun, possessed by a bright madness . . ."—N.Y. Post. ". . . a knockout of original humor."—NBC. ". . . intelligent and very funny play."—WABC-TV.

LITTLE MURDERS
(ALL GROUPS—COMEDY)

By JULES FEIFFER

6 men, 2 women—Interior

"Jules Feiffer, a satirical sharpshooter with a deadly aim, stares balefully at the meaningless violence in American life, and opens fire on it in 'Little Murders.' . . . Can be devastatingly lethal in some of its coldly savage comic assaults." (N.Y. Post). The play is really a collection of what Walter Kerr called set pieces, showing us a modern metropolitan family of matriarchal mother, milquetoast father, normal cuddly sister, and brother who is trying to adapt himself to homosexuality. Sister's fiance is a fellow who knows how to roll with the punches; he figures that if you daydream while being mugged, it won't hurt so much. They have a hard time finding a preacher who will marry them without pronouncing the name of God. But they succeed, to their sorrow. For immediately afterward sister is killed by a sniper's bullet. A detective who has a stack of unsolved crimes suspects that there is "a subtle pattern" forming here. "'Little Murders' is fantastically funny. You will laugh a lot."—N.Y. Times. "You have made me laugh, you have made me collapse. I want to go back."—N.Y. Post. "One of the finest comedies this season.—NBC-TV.

Other Publications for Your Interest

WHITE LIARS
(COMEDY)

By PETER SHAFFER

2 men, 1 woman—Interior

Produced in London and on Broadway as a companion piece to *Black Comedy*. It featured Geraldine Page as a fortune-teller to whom a youth comes with his "buddy" in tow. He doesn't want his fortune told, but he wants to pretend it's been told. What he really wants is to bribe the fortune-teller to frighten his "buddy" so he will relinquish his girl to him. But the "Buddy" sees through the ruse—all the false biography he had planted with the other fellow comes back through the fortune-teller; and both he and the fortune-teller make a discovery about love. "A deft, sharply etched study of three characters."—N.Y. Daily News.

THE PRIVATE EAR AND THE PUBLIC EYE
(LITTLE THEATRE—COMEDY)

By PETER SHAFFER

2 men, 1 woman

Unanimous critical acclaim greeted both the London and Broadway productions of this brace of delightful plays. The first, **The Private Ear**, is a rueful romance in which a boy makes a date with a girl he met at a concert, and has his worldly friend coach him for the occasion. Not only is the coaching all wrong for the occasion, but the girl turns out to be a very rude disappointment. In **The Public Eye** we meet a snappy private detective who dresses like an unmistakable neon sign and is constantly eating yogurt and grapefruit. He has been hired to tail an accountant's wife, but has succeeded in giving himself away every time. "The twin comedies are delightful any way you want to look at them. . . . They are deftly contrived, cheerfully entertaining."—N.Y. Herald Tribune. "They are silky-smooth, literate, witty and irresistibly human."—N.Y. Daily News. "They have in common a most winning quality of humor, sympathy, fresh characterization, imaginative observation and brightly artful entertainment."—N.Y. Post. "At the conclusion of each you know that you have been a guest at two lucid moments of truth."—N.Y. World-Telegram & Sun.

Other Publications for Your Interest

GROWN UPS
(LITTLE THEATRE—COMEDY)

By JULES FEIFFER

2 men, 3 women, 1 female child—Interiors

An acerbic comedy by the famed cartoonist and author of *Knock Knock* and *Little Murders*. It's about a middle-aged journalist who has, at last, grown-up—only to find he's trapped in a world of emotional infants. "A laceratingly funny play about the strangest of human syndromes—the love that kills rather than comforts. Feiffer's vision seems merciless, but its mercy is the fierce comic clarity with which he exposes every conceivable permutation of smooth-tongued cruelty . . . Feiffer constructs a fiendishly complex machine of reciprocal irritation in which Jake (the journalist), his parents, his wife and his sister carp, cavil, harass, hector and finally attack one another with relentless trivia that detonate deeply buried resentments like emotional land mines . . . Moving past Broadway one-liners and easy gags, (Feiffer) makes laughter an adventure . . . This farce is Feiffer's exclusive specialty, and it's never been more harrowingly hilarious."—Newsweek. "Savagely funny."—N.Y. Times. "A compelling, devastating evening of theatre . . . the first adult play of the season."—Women's Wear Daily. (#9125)

LUNCH HOUR
(LITTLE THEATRE—COMEDY)

By JEAN KERR

3 men, 2 women—Interior

Never has Jean Kerr's wit had a keener edge or her comic sense more peaks of merriment than in this clever confection, starring Gilda Radner and Sam Waterston as a pair whose spouses are having an affair, and who have to counter by inventing an affair of their own. He, ironically, is a marriage counsellor, and a bit of a stick. His wife juggles husband, lover and mother and is a real go-getter. In fact, it was she who proposed to him. Of the other couple, the wife is a bit kooky. She can discourse on things tacky while wearing an evening gown with her jogging sneakers on; or, again, be overjoyed at the prospect of a trip to Paris: "And we'll never have to ask for french fried potatoes. They'll just come like that." While her husband, "Well, he's rich for a living." Or as he expresses it: "It's very difficult to do something if you don't need any money." All ends forgivingly for both couples, as the aggrieved wife concedes that they both "need something to regret," and the other husband concedes "I knew when I married that everyone would want to dance with you." "Civilized, charming, stylish . . . Very warm and most amusing . . . delicately interweaves laughter and romance."—N.Y. Times. "An amiable comedy about the eternal quadrangle . . . The author's most entertaining play in years."—N.Y. Daily News. "A beautiful weave of plot, character and laughs . . . It's delicious."—NBC-TV. (#674)

Other Publications for Your Interest

A WEEKEND NEAR MADISON
(LITTLE THEATRE—COMIC DRAMA)
By KATHLEEN TOLAN

2 men, 3 women—Interior

This recent hit from the famed Actors Theatre of Louisville, a terrific ensemble play about male-female relationships in the 80's, was praised by *Newsweek* as "warm, vital, glowing . . . full of wise ironies and unsentimental hopes". The story concerns a weekend reunion of old college friends now in their early thirties. The occasion is the visit of Vanessa, the queen bee of the group, who is now the leader of a lesbian/feminist rock band. Vanessa arrives at the home of an old friend who is now a psychiatrist hand in hand with her naif-like lover, who also plays in the band. Also on hand are the psychiatrist's wife, a novelist suffering from writer's block; and his brother, who was once Vanessa's lover and who still loves her. In the course of the weekend, Vanessa reveals that she and her lover desperately want to have a child—and she tries to persuade her former male lover to father it, not understanding that he might have some feelings about the whole thing. *Time Magazine* heard "the unmistakable cry of an infant hit . . . Playwright Tolan's work radiates promise and achievement."
(#25051)

PASTORALE
(LITTLE THEATRE—COMEDY)
By DEBORAH EISENBERG

3 men, 4 women—Interior
(plus 1 or 2 bit parts and 3 optional extras)

"Deborah Eisenberg is one of the freshest and funniest voices in some seasons."—*Newsweek.* Somewhere out in the country Melanie has rented a house and in the living room she, her friend Rachel who came for a weekend but forgets to leave, and their school friend Steve (all in their mid-20s) spend nearly a year meandering through a mental landscape including such concerns as phobias, friendship, work, sex, slovenliness and epistemology. Other people happen by: Steve's young girlfriend Celia, the virtuous and annoying Edie, a man who Melanie has picked up in a bar, and a couple who appear during an intense conversation and observe the sofa is on fire. The lives of the three friends inevitably proceed and eventually draw them, the better prepared perhaps by their months on the sofa, in separate directions. "The most original, funniest new comic voice to be heard in New York theater since Beth Henley's 'Crimes of the Heart.'"—N.Y. Times. "A very funny, stylish comedy."—The New Yorker. "Wacky charm and wayward wit."—New York Magazine. "Delightful."—N.Y. Post. "Uproarious . . . the play is a world unto itself, and it spins."—N.Y. Sunday Times.
(#18016)

THE GOOD DOCTOR
NEIL SIMON
(All Groups) Comedy
2 Men, 3 Women. Various settings.

With Christopher Plummer in the role of the Writer, we are introduced to a composite of Neil Simon and Anton Chekhov, from whose short stories Simon adapted the capital vignettes of this collection. Frances Sternhagen played, among other parts, that of a harridan who storms a bank and upbraids the manager for his gout and lack of money. A father takes his son to a house where he will be initiated into the mysteries of sex, only to relent at the last moment, and leave the boy more perplexed than ever. In another sketch a crafty seducer goes to work on a wedded woman, only to realize that the woman has been in command from the first overture. Let us not forget the classic tale of a man who offers to drown himself for three rubles. The stories are droll, the portraits affectionate, the humor infectious, and the fun unending.

> "As smoothly polished a piece of work as we're likely to see all season."—*N.Y. Daily News.* "A great deal of warmth and humor —vaudevillian humor—in his retelling of these Chekhovian tales."—*Newhouse Newspapers.* "There is much fun here . . . **Mr. Simon's comic fancy is admirable."—*N.Y. Times.*

(Music available. Write for particulars.)

The Prisoner of Second Avenue
NEIL SIMON
(All Groups) Comedy
2 Men, 4 Women, Interior

Mel is a well-paid executive of a fancy New York company which has suddenly hit the skids and started to pare the payroll. Anxiety doesn't help; Mel, too, gets the ax. His wife takes a job to tide them over, then she too is sacked. As if this weren't enough, Mel is fighting a losing battle with the very environs of life. Polluted air is killing everything that grows on his terrace; the walls of the high-rise apartment are paper-thin, so that the private lives of a pair of German stewardesses next door are open books to him; the apartment is burgled; and his psychiatrist dies with $23,000 of his money. Mel does the only thing left for him to do: he has a nervous breakdown. It is on recovery that we come to esteem him all the more. For Mel and his wife and people like them have the resilience, the grit to survive.

> "Now all this, mind you, is presented primarily in humorous terms."—*N.Y. Daily News.* "A gift for taking a grave subject and, without losing sight of its basic seriousness, treating it with hearty but sympathetic humor . . . A talent for writing a wonderfully funny line . . . full of humor and intelligence . . . Fine fun."—*N.Y. Post.* "Creates an atmosphere of casual cataclysm, and everyday urban purgatory of copelessness from which laughter seems to be released like vapor from the city's manholes."—*Time.*

Other Publications for Your Interest

HUSBANDRY
(LITTLE THEATRE—DRAMA)
By PATRICK TOVATT

2 men, 2 women—Interior

At its recent world premiere at the famed Actors Theatre of Louisville, this enticing new drama moved an audience of theatre professionals up off their seats and on to their feet to cheer. Mr. Tovatt has given us an insightful drama about what is happening to the small, family farm in America—and what this means for the future of the country. The scene is a farmhouse whose owners are on the verge of losing their farm. They are visited by their son and his wife, who live "only" eight hours' drive away. The son has a good job in the city, and his wife does, too. The son, Harry, is really put on the horns of a dilemma when he realizes that he is his folks' only hope. The old man can't go it alone anymore—and he needs his son. Pulling at him from the other side is his wife, who does not want to leave her job and uproot her family to become a farm wife. *Husbandry*, then, is ultimately about what it means to be a *husband*—both in the farm and in the family sense. *Variety* praised the "delicacy of Tovatt's dialogue", and called the play "a literate exploration of family responsibilities in a mobile society." Said *Time*: "The play simmers so gently for so long, as each potential confrontation is deflected with Chekhovian shrugs and silences, that when it boils into hostility it sears the audience."   (#10169)

CLARA'S PLAY
(LITTLE THEATRE—DRAMA)
By JOHN OLIVE

3 men, 1 woman—Exterior

Clara, an aging spinster, lives alone in a remote farmhouse. She is the last surviving member of one of the area's most prominent families. It is summer, 1915. Enter an immigrant, feisty soul named Sverre looking for a few days' work before moving on. But Clara's farm needs more than just a few days' work, and Sverre stays on to help Clara fix up and run the farm. It soon becomes clear unscrupulous local businessmen are bilking Clara out of money and hope to gain control of her property. Sverre agrees to stay on to help Clara keep her family's property. "A story of determination, loyalty. It has more than a measure of love, of resignation, of humor and loyalty."—Chicago Sun-Times. "A playwright of unusual sensitivity in delineating character and exploring human relationships." —Chicago Tribune. "Gracefully-written, with a real sense of place."—Village Voice. A recent success both at Chicago's fine Wisdom Bridge Theatre and at the Great American Play Festival of the world-reknowned Actors Theatre of Louisville; and, on tour, starring Jean Stapleton.   (#5076)